HEAD IN HEAVEN FEET ON EARTH

Parveen Smith

authorHOUSE®

AuthorHouse™ UK
1663 Liberty Drive
Bloomington, IN 47403 USA
www.authorhouse.co.uk
Phone: UK TFN: 0800 0148641 (Toll Free inside the UK)
UK Local: 02036 956322 (+44 20 3695 6322 from outside the UK)

Published by AuthorHouse 02/17/2021

ISBN: 978-1-6655-8562-0 (sc)
ISBN: 978-1-6655-8563-7 (e)

This book is my true story
Dedicated to you as my reader
Continuing the story from
Seeing Is Believing, Believing Is Seeing
With love
Parveen

CONTENTS

~⌇

May The Angels Bring You Peace And Happiness

~⌇

INTRODUCTION

I have been in contact with Angels and the Ascended Masters during my illnesses of breathing difficulties, fibromyalgia and chronic fatigue syndrome. I believe in their support and guidance which has transformed my life forever. Of course, there will still be tests and challenges but life still can be fulfilling. After all tests and challenges are part of our journey.

When we listen to our true feelings, we connect to our inner being. I had received my wake-up call. I was now ready to follow more guidance of how I could serve as a spiritual being and live my life purpose.

Life with my husband and three children on the physical plane was happy because my life on the spiritual planes was connected. I had found something that I had never felt in my life before. It was the unconditional love and support from the angels.

Many will be in search for something missing, many cannot understand why they feel empty and lost. That is simply because they have become disconnected. Yes, disconnected from their spiritual self. Disconnected from the Divine within.

I can say, my life purpose was becoming clearer. And my health still was not good. But that was not a major concern as I now trusted in Divine Will and that all will be well. Time was needed that was all.

Some of us have visions and dreams but they are no ordinary dreams and visions. They connect us to Divine communication. Be it for guidance for the future or a message of support. My visions were becoming regular. The communication was definitely coming really thick and fast. For an ordinary person this was to some extent mind blowing but it was all happening for a reason. I had already received my wake–up call and it was definitely felt. My body was in shock on the physical level but spiritually

I was being woken up. The illness needed to happen. As I write this book now it is very clear.

Many days and nights I would wonder what had I done so wrong to be paying the price of almost dying as it felt to me. I had no control over my physical body, it was just so weak. Eating and breathing was difficult at the same time for me and yet I was to appreciate little things a lot more. The time to stop and empathise with the suffering of the world around me. The world that is so far and yet so near. My sensitivity had gone up another level. And all I had to do was to listen to it.

Just listen to your body it does speak to you.

xxx

Before I continue my journey from 2006, I have an easy grounding method you could do before you read on.

AN EASY METHOD OF GROUNDING

Grounding is being anchored to the physical planes, the earth.

It is important to be grounded to mother earth so that one does not feel floaty or out of the body. You can close your eyes to do this, after you have read it a few times.

- Imagine you are a strong oak tree.
- Your body is the trunk of the tree.
- Your feet are the roots of the tree.
- Visualise the roots going deep into the core of mother earth.
- Affirm to yourself –I am grounded.
- The tree is rooted.
- You are grounded.
- If you cannot visualise affirm with intention that you are grounded.

CHAPTER 1

~~~*Was I To Believe Everything He Told Me*~~~

As my story continues, it was as if I was playing a part in a movie. And they were up there watching me. You may wonder who I'm talking about. All will be revealed.

I had been seeing a spiritual healer whom told me through each healing that I needed to stand in my own power. He told me about my links with Atlantis. He could see mermaid like connections. He even talked about other high beings having connections with me. He once said I had a deep connection with Mother Meera. Connection with an Avatar where there is no separation. A divine being who has incarnated. He said let the Divine Mother energies work through me. Just allow. He kept saying we were as the one. He saw me in her and her within me. The next visit I took an old photo of me and he saw the exact resemblance. To be truthful I could see it to a certain point. How bizarre. What was this all meaning? He said I would hear Angels more and more. The Angels will strongly guide me to make my dreams come true. At this time, I found all this information very exciting. He also told me to be aware of some family members. Now this was also interesting. It was like, someone as a wolf in sheep's clothing. I sort of understood this message. I was on my guard now. But one thing this person said to me left me a bit startled. A bit? Very. He said something would happen to my husband when he would be 45 years old. I thought, what is going to happen? Is he going to die? I was left uncomfortable. I can remember then telling my friends Lyn and Caroline about this. They said it was rather strange.

~~~*Amazing Incidences*~~~

There was one incident Where I had been helping my niece whom was imbalanced due to her age. For her that was a vulnerable time. I asked my sister how she was doing. She said she was somewhat better. I asked my mother how my niece was getting along too; the outcome was good less attacks. She may not need medication.

~⌣

During these times I was now amazed more and more as Tristen my son, saw a boy outside the house near our front door. But when we looked out, there was no body there. At this same time there I saw a figure playing hide and seek. It was a young person but when we looked closely to see who they were and where they went, there was nothing there. A couple of days later, my daughter heard a female call her voice when she looked around no one was there. Daren my husband heard a female call his name in the kitchen but he was the only one in there. Now the family were sensing much more. The spirits, be it angels or those whom had passed were making their presence.

~⌣

There had now come a time where Daren and my brother -in-law Paul were on Ebay for auction. The site was called Auction Angel 72. It was for some walking boots. We were amazed. The item was placed for £81 but then all of a sudden Daren said to me ask your angels to get me these boots. I had already asked for help but then I said you ask if you really want the boots. He asked in his own way. I reminded him to say thank you. We watched the bidding. The boots sold to Daren for £33. It was truly unbelievable. The sacred number connecting to Divine source is 3.

~⌣

Alysha my youngest daughter saw a boy peeping into the living room whom was not in the physical body. But she could clearly see him. She said he was Tristen's age. She said the name Michael came to her. Then she said Archangel Michael, I thought Archangel Michael cannot be a boy.

Alysha saw him peep in again. I was discussing this with Daren. Tristen then said out loud he had seen a boy with brown hair peeping over the smaller window at the side of the house. Just where I had seen few days previously. Tristen confirmed the boy was around his age. Interesting as we were all seeing and hearing.

~

I had recently been let down by someone I trusted. I sat in my conservatory meditating on this cold January morning the sun shone through which gave a pleasant feel to the day. I was shown a male walking away. Then a red rose appeared, a bird and a lotus. I knew these symbols were spiritual. I was also receiving the message 'with love fly freely, have courage'. My intuition was also confirming that Christ energy was present. Towards the end of the meditation the crucifix appeared.

Then a couple of nights later the bird in flight was reappearing in my night vision. I was again receiving the similar message, 'Set free, flying high'. The image of the thumbs up appeared just like weeks previously. I was not scared but excited. Just waiting to see what was in store for me was great. I suppose you could say I was embarking on a spiritual adventure. It was the mystery of spirit. The very same night a male voice spoke it only revealed the word 'serpent'. The serpents spiritual meaning is more than one, someone whom may betray you, or shedding the skin like a snake going through transformations.

After sometime I was shown an underwater scene. It was beautiful, the whales gliding effortlessly. Nearby were also sharks and other fish.

~

Because I felt I had lost the trust, in a person who was supposed to support me, I think I did feel in some sense vulnerable. The message with this vision was telling me to protect myself and to discern anything that did not feel right for me. Also, that there were expansive opportunities out on the physical and spiritual planes. After this vision had faded, I was then shown paradise. The enriched green palm trees with the glowing of sun rays and pure golden sands.

∾

The next day I needed some healing I could not get in touch with Dorothea so I knew of another healer I would like to have healing from. He was willing to see me that very day. As I arrived at the home of this person we chatted. S made me comfortable and soon started the healing. I felt his six-foot spirit guide assist the session. It was different to what I had experienced with any other healer. As S placed his hands on my back, I instantly knew that this was not him giving the healing. The breathing of the guide had changed it was much heavier. It did not frighten me but I knew I was just to trust. I would need to do that so I could proceed with life. Holding on to past let downs or mistrust was not healthy but my experience of being let down had only just happened, with being a sensitive soul extra spiritual support was required right now. I returned home and was ready for a good rest.

~~~Finding My Publishers~~~

A few days later in my sleep I was woken to be shown a desk and a keyboard. The visual then went on to a couple of rabbits, they were playing happily. The message I was now receiving was to be creative and write. Now this was the push to investigate who would be my publisher for my first book and to start to write. Without a doubt my visions were my guidance. I was urged to get a move on. I knew it would be a big task to start looking for a publisher. After sitting in contemplation, I pulled out my local yellow pages from Daren's granddads old side board which was almost a hundred years old. I needed to find which publishing firms were in my locality for my very first book. After phoning a few they were not interested. Then I contacted some major publishing firms but the telephone line was disconnected. Strange, I thought as I was dialling UK numbers. Feeling down hearted and frustrated I thought of leaving it until the morning. As I felt dejected, I walked towards the kitchen when suddenly the music in the conservatory came on by itself. It was the angels' music. I then knew I just needed to relax, and that was exactly what I did. That evening I asked the angels for their guidance and support to help me find the right publishing company.

Waking up early the very next morning to darkness I entered the bathroom. The window was misty with condensation as I glared, I could see writing. The condensated window was holding a vital message. It was the answer to my question the previous night. I could not quite believe my eyes as I glanced harder at the window. Visibly it was quite clear. What was scribed was 'Jean Kelford', with a 'T' underneath it. This was one of the authors at the 'second sight' night I went to see months previously. Amazed as usual, I called Sharon to have a look at what was on the window. We both watched the condensated message dribble to the ledge. I then went into my bedroom and picked up Jean's book from the bookshelf and searched for the meaning of 'T'. Yes, there it was a 'T' for Trafford, the publishing company. As soon as the children went to school, I wasted no time. I telephoned Trafford and chatted to D he advised me with which packages were possibly suitable for my book. As he did so I explained how I had not worked for a while due to ill health and that I had raised some funds but would need to raise more. He was very understanding and managed to speak to his boss to enable me to take the best possible package for my work. A feel of amazing love was felt over the airwaves. I expressed to this individual that I could feel something great. He agreed with me. We both said it was an amazing feeling of pure love. This person had also recently embarked on a spiritual journey. There was definitely a connection. I knew I was doing the right thing and decided to make an agreement with Trafford. I had to tell someone about my new venture as I was left with profound love that almost came from nowhere. I telephoned Paula, Daren's cousin, to tell her, she just listened as I spoke in excitement. The pure love remained with me for the rest of that day. Looking back at the scribbled notes the time I had made that phone call to Trafford was at 9.13 am. The time for me was significant; The Divine Truth of God and the number of Ascended Masters of keeping trust and faith.

~~~Trusting The Messages~~~

I had now met H an ex-colleague of mine for a chat and a catch up as we had not spoken for a while. She seemed somewhat amazed as I read her cards for her. This was not what I would normally do but there was a reason as to why I needed to give her guidance. She was a little spooked. I knew though that she needed to make changes this was not something she could just push aside.

Others who were already receiving guidance from me needed to have reassurance about the things that were happening. After discussing what the way forward was the problem resolved itself.

~

I had received a message from Angel Pagiel that I was now committing myself to where my life path was taking me. I had already signed my agreement and was writing my first book. This angel was reassuring me that I was receiving pure guidance. Angel Geniel was also giving me the push towards my destiny as my visions had already appeared weeks previously.

I was now being told to put closure to something that had misaligned me. I knew exactly what it was. I needed to forget that I had been left in the lurch by somebody I trusted. I just needed to move on and continue my renewed passion. Many people will be going through what I have and I am not the first. Journey on the spiritual path is beautiful but testing at times. Nevertheless, it was that special feeling I had felt whilst on my journey.

My vision that I had this very night was beautiful as it told me of the beauty around me. It was as if I was seeing myself looking out of a window to a beautiful colourful scene of the trees. Yes, still unwell but it was not my focus any more as I had reached a point in my life where I was told not to give up and that my soul would not let me. The angels and masters would not let me. My job was not done. I had not served my purpose in life.

The two towers or aligned pillars that I was shown represent strength and beauty. Or a gateway, a portal awaiting.

The animal spirits; seal and polar bear were also telling me that I needed to write everyday which is what I was trying to do. My dreams were becoming vivid and the challenges I had faced were coming to an end. I was now to stay focused on the task before me as more of my hidden gifts were to emerge.

The night vision I received on this February in the early hours of the morning was reassuring for I could see it clearly.

The candle is a symbol of peace and healing. It is the eternal flame, the light. The nature spirits were also calling to take time out in nature to get the fresh air that was needed to revitalise me. The horse was also telling me of the power that I have, and not to fear the use of it. The fishes and whales in the vast deep blue ocean were all swimming in harmony. Some big fish and some small, beautiful coloured fish were gliding effortlessly in the same direction as everything was to go with the flow. The scale of the large whale was peacefully going with the flow; it was a privilege to receive this image of the underwater life. I woke up the next morning with an angel blessing stuck to my face. Alysha my youngest daughter and I laughed.

The very next night I asked God what I needed to know. I was shown the ocean again with fish swimming and then a baby with wings. The baby was swimming underwater happily. The message was clear to me as I was told I was the baby in a big ocean. During my meditation in the afternoon the fox was already revealing to me that there was someone who was trying to trick me in some way but also not to be outrun by them.

Well, how bizarre as only yesterday I had an angel blessing stuck to my face and today I had a silver confetti star in my bed.

~

During another night vision I was shown dinosaurs, mainly tyrannosaurus rex, what was this meaning for me? Then I received a symbol, the information I was given was that I had received ancient spiritual insight. The rabbit was telling me not to be afraid. I was also shown my ladies business shoe and a walking boot. I was told to walk the walk. Walk the business. It was no good to sit thinking about it, I was meant to do it. Maybe there was more of a message or guidance with this vision.

~

I had now been facilitating angel evenings that could be enlightening for those interested. T had come to the evening to listen and share. Obviously, a Christian in his belief and he was intrigued I suppose you could say. T had come for a healing session to see if it could help him with his fibromyalgia, but he also had a medical heart condition. Being aware of his condition I hoped everything would be all right. I knew I wanted him to experience angel healing because that is what he came for. We discussed how T was going to receive the angel healing, making sure he was comfortable. I had also told him to let me know if he wanted to stop at any time. The healing was going well until about half way through he said he felt pains in his left side of his body. At that precise moment I also felt chest pain almost as if I had been shot in the chest. My heart was pounding as he raised his hand. I closed down the healing as numbness followed in my arm. With T's permission I placed my hand over his left arm where he could feel the pain shooting down to his hand. As I did this, he actually felt the pain subside. At this point this gentleman had tears in his eyes. We discussed how he felt. He did say that he was emotional but wouldn't usually show his emotions in that way. As he held back his tears, I knew that profound healing had taken place for him. He was left sitting in awe and astonishment. The power that I have is not all mine it is Divine and for use of highest good of others.

The very next day my vision was somewhat different of the ocean scene. The scene was still in colour with the same backdrop. The vision was now showing small fishes being eaten by the big fishes. Truthfully, I did not like the image but it was there for a reason. My next vision followed straight after showing me a sheriff wearing his beige uniform, I could see his six-pointed sheriff's badge with 'sheriff' written on it. The place was clearly a jail as I could see the bars. He was dangling a set of heavy, bundle of keys. Looking at me to say you can be free if you want to, take the opportunity. This was now showing me that I am the boss. I have the keys. An intuitive message also came to light as I was told that 'I have the keys to alchemy.' I was shown the image twice. They were making sure I was receiving the message. I was no longer to be a prisoner; I was to be free. I lay in contemplation when this message was for. I believed that it was for the future months. As already I had discovered on my journey not all spiritual people are all that they can be, or did not fulfil their role. I would need to take these visions into consideration as to when the situations arise. I would need to use my discernment; this will make sense later. During this same night my dream revealed that Daren was shocked with my abilities and that of the angelic beings. In the dream he had seen things moving before his own eyes. I believe he will see more one day only when the time is right for him.

~

The next night I was shown the military officer, it was the cowboy sheriff being blessed with the sword as he knelt down. It was a sight of upgrading for the sheriff, which resonated with me.

~

The messages were definitely guidance. In the early hours of the morning this next vision was in pure gold. The number '4' appeared first, then wings of love and then a phoenix. The phoenix was all about transformation and moving forward with love from the angels. As I was now already an angel healing practitioner, this made sense. I was then shown dull rain clouds, which did not sound too promising. The nature spirits that came through next would be my support and guidance. Next, I was shown angel wings and I was intuitively told that Archangel Michael would assist me and protect me during my transformations and then the phoenix returned in full sight what a beautiful sight. After having a little more sleep, I was woken up at 4.55 to be shown a lion and a bear. Then appeared in my vision a bungalow and the word 'transformation.' During this time, I was also shown the image of my present house, subsequently my smaller house appeared that in which we lived in prior to the one we are in now. After this I heard the voice of a female whom I knew of in the physical world. The words were not clear but the voice was definitely hers. The intuitive message that was given was 'now and then.' I was being shown where I am now and where I was then. The messages were coming through fast now, I was told not to hold back and to spread my wings and I would understand more of the spiritual teachings. My career goals would also shift as my energies had changed from the person I was prior, to opening up spiritually now. When one becomes ready to receive spiritual understandings and follows their path anything is possible. I had already started to receive esoteric symbols but unaware of their meaning they would come in beautiful shapes and moving just like a kaleidoscope.

~

I still had not recovered from the fibromyalgia and chronic fatigue but was very happy in an inward meaning. My spirit was much happier and freer. I understood a lot more spiritually about life so I did not feel I needed to moan and groan about anything. I suppose I just trusted that one day not too far away I would recover.

I had now decided to look for somewhere to work from as the angels were guiding me to work from a public setting and to spread my wings. Even if it was an hour a day. I was to help those who needed freeing from the materialistic unhappy lives, so that there could be balance for the soul. I felt I could take the angel healing to the public. Some may want spiritual healing for growth on their own journey or for those wanting help for mental, emotional or physical conditions.

~

This particular day I went to see my doctor and I wanted to tell him that I had now decided to work a little as that was what I was guided to do by the angels. He did ask how I felt in myself and he did know that I had not recovered. The doctor could also see that I was determined to fulfil my mission. He sat and listened attentively and then shook my hand and thanked me for my decision. He wished me all the best and understood that was what I wanted to do. At that moment I felt I had his blessings too.

That very evening, I received another esoteric symbol which meant that 'I was receiving spiritual understanding and assistance from the spiritual world.'

After my visit with the gentle and caring doctor I did more angel guidance cards for myself and they told me to stay optimistic about my life as there are magical opportunities for self employment and a new location for my new job. As I continue to follow my life mission work there will be great improvements for my life and for others.

~

The next night my vision was again telling me of the number '4', the horse shoe that was a lucky one was now broken. This again was not a very comforting thought as I felt I was to face some disappointments. Straight after I was shown a big boot it was a flat lady's boot but quite high and long fitting. I was also shown roots as if they would be flowing into the ground. I then saw the arrow facing upwards. Fish were swimming in the same direction. I knew that meant go with the flow. I was also told that I would need to remain grounded and to rise above the problem. Just swim with the flow. Not long after I could see a kangaroo jumping. The kangaroo was telling me that all would be fine as the angels would look after me and to continue what I was doing.

CHAPTER 2

~~~Setting Up My Healing Space~~~

It was only a few days to go now before I started my first day in a clinic to provide the service of angel healings. Well, the business place was a bungalow with a horseshoe on the side of the bungalow and the number 4. With amazement yet again but knowing I was in the flow. I was quite excited and knew that this would be a new challenge but one I would enjoy as my true, heartfelt desires lay in this service. It had been a few days since my last vision or guidance. I made preparation for meditation. As usual I would cleanse the area I would be sitting in, ensuring there would be no lower energies. I entered my calm stillness of sitting and then I started feeling intense vibrations running through my entire body. Starting from the crown chakra and following to my feet. The vibrations were that strong that my whole body was shaking. It was strange but I did not feel frightened as I knew this would only be from The Divine. My purpose had been accepted. I suppose I felt comfortable to a certain degree that all was safe. At this time, I also felt that I was levitating, quite aware of my surroundings as I could hear the children downstairs. I then received a grid like symbol with crosses inside it. This meant that I had a gift of partnerships for all things and the union with my own divine self. I was very privileged as I had been told through my visions that I would receive more esoteric information.

~

Because I had now accepted my life mission, I knew that God was giving me more as spiritual concepts. I was feeling unconditional love and support and simply knew it was coming from above. The feeling of gratitude and honour was within my entire being.

The very next day I received another grid like symbol and they had actually got circles in them. I was told by this symbol that it was about individuality and having the drive, the confidence and leadership over situations. The triangle appeared in my vision and an eye with a beam of light. Now I was being told that I had gifts and talents that would benefit others without too much effort. I had reached the stage of carrying the good karma. It actually was from other life times, so I just needed to reach this part of my life to realise that I had not quite finished off my role in other life times.

～

In another night vision I had seen an eagle claw then emerged the beautiful eagle telling me about my passion for life. Straight after a native American-Indian man appeared and then the eagle soared. I believe I was privileged to meet a native spirit guide. The next evening the vision that came through was of a beautiful Egyptian Princess and Talos was guarding the ancient treasures. Talos a one horned giant being, stood guarding, holding his golden spear. The peace was to follow as I was shown a white dove and butterflies and angels. The significant meaning of transformations as the angels would be my support through my future. I was then told that 'through transformation peace is brought to you from the angels.' My shoes that I would wear for business where shown, then the image of the fish swimming away from the whale were also shown. A reminder that in business I may have to walk away from someone bigger than myself.

～

As Si made contact and arrived for his healing, he enjoyed the unique experience of receiving guidance. I will call him Si in this story, a tall grounded lovely person. A spiritual guy searching for his life path. He surely did receive what he came for as a voice spoke to him. Again, no guarantee can be given as to any outcome, patience is required and when one is meant to receive from a higher source they will do so. This man had his connections in Egypt as I could see him with a camel. Si was pleased with his first meeting with me and was looking forward for another session at some point soon. That same evening Si was out on his duty in the evening as he explained he saw a small white angel orb. He felt calm as well as pleased for this sighting. That very night I too had received a message for Si from the angels. The voice was that of a female she spoke beautifully giving this message 'To pray for what he wants to do in life, he will get help.' Then I was shown a pair of hands praying. I was only too happy to share this message with Si. He obviously appreciated it.

~

A couple of nights later I received the rune arrows one displaying up and next to it one was pointing down. They were actually telling me that I had the courage and to be confident that situations would improve. The animal spirit bear was telling me that I needed to set clear boundaries about my creative projects whether at home or in business. I had made clear what I wanted to do with those around me and professionally, as the angels wanted me to take my work to a public level. I woke up one morning feeling very much guided by the angels to hold an Angel Evening in a public setting. So, whilst out for dinner one evening I was speaking to a gentleman about the work that I did and before you knew it the evening was agreed from his premises. When I was in this public setting, I met a waitress who had become very emotional whilst in my presence. She bowed her head and tears flowed down her cheek. She began to say that there was something very different about me. As she reached in her pocket for a tissue, I told her she was feeling the presence of an angel, this was my angel. She said she had never felt the pure loving feeling in her life. As she hugged me, I then felt a part of her nervous energy transmitting into my body. A few days later I went into the restaurant to finalise details and the same lady had again, said she felt something from me and that she had the best nights sleep ever.

This same day Master Djwhal Khul had appeared, his message was telling me; healing for others and that many were receiving healing in my presence. This is what people meeting me were telling me.

~~~*Karma*~~~

I had been to my local spiritualist church one Sunday evening with Paula. In this room I was definitely sensing lots of emotional distress from those whom had lost loved ones. Even the occasional shadow of a spirit passed by as I spoke to Paula. There was perhaps another reason for being at this evening. I was drawn to a lady. She walked in earlier and sat down near to us. I really wanted to speak to her about her son's death, she seemed so desperately in need of comfort. The evening ended and everyone left quite quickly. I felt I had to contact her about her son who had passed away years ago due to a very tragic death. I went to the grave of this teenager and a left a note for the mother. That night I had a spirit making contact and I knew this was the son. My vision of the dove of peace landing on a very large hand confirmed to me that night that all this soul wanted was peace and will be there soon. However, the lady did not contact me but what I wanted to tell her was that justice will be done what goes round comes round. She was obviously very devastated. I had this sense of what happened to her son would happen to the culprits. Only weeks later I was told that the culprit died in a tragic accident similar to the way the teenager died. How did this actually happen? For me it's almost like I am told inwardly something is going to happen. No one wants to hear awful things happening but I do believe it was Karma. Astounded I was when I received the telephone call. I just hoped the mother of the son could rest a little even though this was tragic what happened to the boys.

~

The animal spirits were making their regular contact bringing various messages. The wolf, the baboon and even my own gorilla animal spirit Onch appeared, his message was 'just soaring' I could see him walking on all fours in a beautiful jungle.

~~~*Alone In The House*~~~

Daren had gone on a walking trip, he was away from home which meant it was just me and my children.

In the middle of the night a figure of a large male dressed in black stood at the right side of my bed. I am sure I was half awake. This figure was not a physical entity but an entity of some kind. Yes, I had become frightened. It was actually pulling the duvet of me and then I fought with it. It was not funny at the time. I was not going to give in to it. There was no chance of that, it was not a pleasant entity I can assure readers. Where it had come from, I do not know. I insisted it could do no harm and called upon the angels, Jesus Christ and God. I recited this for some time to come, that only the love and light of the angels were around me.

My vision that appeared soon was of Anubis the Egyptian Dog God dressed in a security uniform. I could see the security badge shining as his black uniform stood out. He looked fearsome but I knew he was a protector of some kind. He was checking the house with a torch. I could see my whole house lit in a pure white glow. This vision appeared twice just to ensure that I received the message of protection. I must admit I felt a little better.

The next night I was shown a parent angel holding a younger angel in her arms, they were both levitating. The unicorn appeared again just like months previously. The message was surely a link with parents and special gifted children.

~~~Angel Messages~~~

The reminder was coming again that someone will try and trick me in some way but it will be in my power to see ahead and take the leadership role for the future. The angel appearing in my vision explained all this to me.

The next day I felt fearful, I had no reasoning for this as I felt protected by Anubis. I did some self-healing and the feeling went away.

A couple of nights earlier I held one of my angel evenings and some of the audience felt emotional healing taking place and one lady felt the heartburn she had for several years leave her during her time with me. Her message came back via her cousin that her symptoms had gone. She was however very reluctant to go and see her doctor in case it was serious. Since that day this lady has had no further problems since receiving presence healing. What I call presence healing was just sitting in the room and I felt healing coming through me to others. Others that had attended the evenings had felt emotional release, their spiritual awareness growing and more able to speak their truth.

Jackie was a lady whom attended the Angel Evening and I had given options for some of them to stay behind for a one-to-one reading. Jackie had a card reading from me. The answers she needed were clear for her. She was guided to go ahead and do the course. My smoke detectors started bleeping too. I felt this was confirmation on the reading. She left feeling clearer about her decisions.

After this evening I went to bed like I normally would relaxing into sleep state but I was woken up at 4.33 am. I could see a spiritual romantic relationship, a dove, parent angel and child angel, unicorn, crocodile and a fox catching white doves. I still found it an unsettling night. The messages waking me up, maybe also of what happened the night before with the dark figure. I could see more symbols, a horse and father healing symbol from one of Doreen Virtue cards for guidance. I was now being told that there will be a new level of romantic relationship coming in for me. Parent and child are connected like angels. The unicorn was the message of helping children with special abilities. The crocodile was showing how someone will call me in the future, I will need strength, watch out for any cunningness, it could be a time of magic, strength and bravery will be needed. The fox was someone who is cunning and not wanting me to be in peace, or even destroying the peace that once was. This sounds strange; I may need to come back to this message.

In the morning I could still see romantic people. A deer also was given to me for a message. This animal was telling me to work through any obstacles with grace. Be vigilant as a course of direction may need to be looked at. I have the magical abilities to regenerate and come back to understanding mystery of my life path.

~

Sarah had been coming for regular healings and things in her life had changed and she was ready for transformations. Her time in her present employment was done. She had come for some healing due to an interview. The messages were strong as she was to go ahead and work with some autistic children. It would be challenging but spiritually she needed to go ahead with this role of working with those children who are gifted but unrecognised as who they really are. They need the support of those who can truly understand them. These souls are sensitive and need guidance from mature souls they can connect with. I truly felt that the guidance that was coming was to assist Sarah to a new way of thinking and to teach her about the new children of our future. They are here to make a statement.

CHAPTER 3

~~~My Calling To The Next Level~~~

It was now the months of spring. I had taken my work out to a public setting. I felt it would take a little time for those people to find their way for angel healings to me as the angels would guide them. In the meantime, I needed time to write my very first book and any extra time was dedicated to doing just that.

The post had arrived and I opened a white envelope inside was a leaflet from Rosemary, the lady I did the angel healing course with the previous September. The leaflet was for the Masters Course. As soon as I had started to read it my heart beat became faster and faster with an overwhelming feeling of joy. As I was reading the leaflet, I felt the powerful energies calling me. As soon as I finished reading it, I burst into tears. The feeling was indescribable, almost too powerful for words. It felt I was being called urgently to do the master's course. The love, the joy, well, the call was overwhelming as I sobbed for a further five minutes. I then shouted at the top of my voice that I was coming, I was on my way to do my duty. I spoke to Lyn my friend to tell her about my experience with a leaflet. But it was no ordinary happening. The vibrations from the Angelic Kingdom were intense and remained with me for the rest of the day. Wei-ling an ex-colleague arrived for her healing she was mithered with losing her house keys, she looked everywhere and they were not found. I was telling Wei-Ling that the angels wanted her to lighten up a bit and to have a laugh. As she listened her telephone rang and it was a giggly tone. She was only to find out that a pupil had them in her coat pocket. This was confirming all what I was saying. After she had found her keys we laughed.

~

The visions I received at night were telling me that spirits, angels, fairies and archangels were around me. Someone once said that they would only be visible at the beginning of my journey but I know that they have never left my side.

Again, the many animal spirits were coming through during my daily meditation. This could be because my guardian angel was Ariel who is the Archangel of nature and courage and standing for beliefs.

The next day I received an unusual telephone call from the person who had abandoned me and surprised I was to hear an apology. The sort of person that I am, I don't like to make people feel awkward so I was about to say that all was fine and it was alright. As I tried to open my mouth, I felt gagged. There was a definite restriction as I could not verbalise. I now realise that it was due to the fact that it would not be truthful to say it was ok. Also, the angels gagged me because an apology was to be made. Here is an example of how the angels can interact even with or without words. Or should I say no words. I do understand that it was necessary for both of us, that I was gagged and couldn't speak and the other person needed to make that apology. My personal power was in my hands and the animal spirits message came through of being strong and to maintain respect for myself. It was quite strange as in my night vision I also saw a digger which was linking in with the work that was being done in my road. Again, I knew that each vision meant something for me and amazed still to see the link.

~~~Trip To Scotland~~~

Daren had planned his next trip to Scotland. Tristen was to join him on the walking expedition. Alysha and I had booked in to stay at Tyndrum in a bed and breakfast. As soon as I had made the booking with Angie, I knew I was choosing the right place to be. Even getting an additional night free. As I meditated on the train, I could see white cottages. We arrived at Dalkell cottages by taxi. When I arrived at our destination, I was pleasantly surprised to see the white cottages were Dalkell as I smiled to myself as it was my confirmation through meditation. I knew I was supposed to come here, it was that sense of comfort and belonging. Mr Slater had been very helpful as Daren and Tristen had barely minutes to catch their last train to their destination in daylight. Because where they were going was just so rural in the middle of nowhere. Mr Slater gave Daren and Tristen a lift to the railway station. We stayed in room 5 and I couldn't believe what I saw hanging on the bedroom wall. It was the same picture of Buchaille Etive Mor as we have in our bedroom. I also noticed in the lounge there was a movie of Jesus Christ I had made plans to watch this over the time of our stay. In my bedroom that night I saw orange, red and blue angel lights another comfort of knowing that we were not alone. Alysha was due for some healing and this was the perfect place. She lay on the bed and I felt the healing take place in her body. She felt pain in her arms, legs and stomach. She also saw fairies. She said how they had formed a circle above her brow. And she could also see a queen fairy with her tiara on her head. What a lovely way to end the night. We both slept rather well.

After breakfast I decided to watch the Jesus movie. I had confirmations that we should follow his teachings. I even became emotional as I feel a deep connection with Jesus.

Alysha and I walked along the small forest area by the stream. It was a beautiful area the trees shadowing the sky view and the sun rays flowing in on us occasionally. The air was extremely fresh. I inhaled the crispness of it and felt energised. A few highland walkers crossed our path as we watched the exhaustion in them. The little forest area was the route of the highland walk. I took my boots off and put my feet in the stream to cleanse out on this spring morning. The water was actually quite cold. Alysha threw stones into the stream and happily played whilst I closed my eyes just to meditate for a few minutes. I felt very calm and serene at this point. After all there was no rush and no sense of time.

We had a lovely time together of watching the world go by. The continuous arrival of coaches stopping bringing tourists in for lunch. The tiny birds waiting on the wall for peoples left over food. They weren't a nuisance it was just lovely to see them. The bikers were in groups enjoying the beautiful spring weather., riding through showing off their particular bikes.

In the night I had physical pain as if it was heart attacks. I knew this pain related to a male and worried if Tristen and Daren were all right. I could not contact them as there was no reception on the mobile phone. I however did worry that night.

We took it steady at breakfast as I did not sleep well and felt fatigued. As Angie tidied the breakfast table I sat and meditated in a chair near to the window. The sun shone in; it was beautiful. I kept seeing the number 59, and number 4. I could feel that I was connecting with higher energies with the pale shades of gold's and pinks. Well, it was the first day of April but I was sure that the number could be Angie's age. Later that morning I did ask her and yes, it was her age. Angie had also told me about the perfume aromas she has smelt that are like no other she has smelt before. She enquired could it be the angels I was getting the confirmation to her question and explained that was so.

Alysha and I walked towards the bottom of a mountain; it took us a while as I needed regular rests. Alysha was very aware of my fibromyalgia and the chronic fatigue which could appear or even worsen at any stage. It was great to feel a sense of freedom in the middle of almost nowhere. The West Highland Way continued through this area. We saw groups of people of all ages walking through. I lay on the grass and started to connect with the Mahatma energies, the tingling overwhelmed me form my feet towards the top of my legs. Once again it was that tranquillity. We enjoyed our time, just us girls.

Daren and Tristen had joined us that last evening. We enjoyed our meal together and then returned to our rooms.

We caught our train to Glasgow station and boarded fifteen minutes early to ensure we had four seats together. The train manager had given the children an activity pack. They needed it as it was a long journey home. Daren sat next to me, as Alysha sat next to Tristen. Across the way sat a lady. I instantly knew that someone she knew had died. I heard her sobbing and wanted to instantly go and help her. I asked Daren to kindly move so that I could speak to this lady. He really did not want me to do this and did not agree with moving. So, I had to get a little annoyed with him so that he would move.

I could hear her sobbing quite loudly by this stage. I asked if she was all right, knowing full well she was not but it is always that difficult moment of finding the right words to say when someone is so distressed. I told her I knew it was something serious. She sobbed whilst telling me her boyfriend had suddenly died. I offered her some tissues and held her hand. As I too took a deep sigh. I could feel tears in my eyes too but what good would I be if I sat there sobbing too as I felt her emotions. I sat with her for a further ten minutes until her telephone rang and then left her talking to her loved ones. The shock was all too much for this lady. Repeatedly her mobile telephone rang and again and again she sobbed as she tried to speak. I asked the lady if she wanted a coffee as it could help her.

She welcomed my offer. I bought us both a drink and a chocolate. Knowing that she would be peckish at some point, she was grateful for what I had done. For me it was a normal act as it was my intuition guiding me so. We sat and chatted briefly as she was still in so much shock. She said she had just arrived at Glasgow and now was on the next train back to London after hearing the dreadful news. It was a terrible ordeal to go through. I asked her if she had someone to meet her in London, she said she had family waiting. After a while I left her to come to terms with what had happened but she sobbed all the way on the train. Many passengers had noticed her sobbing too. After a while I found the train manager in another carriage and told her about the lady and asked what she could do to help her. The manager was aware of her sobbing but had also noticed I was sitting with her. She offered to escort the lady to first class so that she could have privacy. The manager made the staff aware and made the lady comfortable. Afterwards the manager said I could go and sit with her if I wanted. And that she would also let the next manager of the train know as she was coming to the end of her shift and would be alighting before us. I was very thankful to the manager. After a short while I ventured along the fast-running carriages to see if the lady was feeling all right. I asked her if I could sit next to her and she moved her coat to make room for me. I told her that I had an experience a couple of nights ago and felt terrible chest pains and knew it related to a male. She said her boyfriend did have chest pains a few nights ago. I now had this feeling that this young male, the same age as Daren had a heart attack. She said how she loved him and had been together for a few years. All she repeated was I cannot believe he has gone. I told her how I already knew I was supposed to help her. I told her about my connection with the angels. I asked her if she believed in angels and God. She said that she did not believe but one thing she did believe that her boyfriend had sent me to help her. She hugged me and thanked me. I felt compelled to give her a crystal and some angel blessings that I had in my bag and I dowsed them with the aura essence to give her the extra support she needed. I told her to sit with the crystal in her hand until she arrived at her destination. She thanked me and said I was an angel. Her words were very touching. I wish I could have done more but I trust that the angels guided me to her and my job was done. That evening I saw the young man's name in a vision and then I felt he was trying to make contact, but I was already too tired.

~~~*Mahatma Energies*~~~

The next day I meditated and I was automatically feeling Mahatma energies coming through. It is a powerful energy and a slightly different vibration to what I am already used to. I thanked Jesus Christ for everything and told him that I was devoted and of service, simultaneously I wept. I knew I was again receiving his blessing.

During the night I felt very ill. My heart was beating fast and there was a lot of surges of vibration passing through my body. The way I understand this is that my own vibration was changing for my future service and indeed it was powerful enough to knock me of my feet.

∽

In the month of April with Easter soon approaching, the weather was overcast and mild. The day was Good Friday. In my meditation I was shown my family and my summer sandals, it was that reminder that I need to spend time away with my family as a balance of working and pleasure.

During the days healing I could see a book, this was not the first time I could see this book. The words were visible. It was amazing because it felt like I was actually reading this book, however I do not know what the book is. This actually is no ordinary book either. It is in the form of scrolls the scroll is long with English text as far as I could understand it. The word **immortal** was clearly shown to me. Some faces appeared in the healing, faces that I did not recognise but then there was a face of someone very special and very well respected. It was Martin Luther King, he was shown in his mid thirties with his head tilted slightly and his soft brown skin shining as he stared with a slight smile to his face. The words that followed were **wise–wisdom-God.** Wow, mmm…….. what was I to make of this? An incredible vision to say the least. Honouring that this powerful energy could come to me was what crossed my mind initially. Overall, it is beautiful that without ever thinking of great leaders such as Mahatma Gandhi and Martin Luther king that they appear to give strong messages. I appreciated by now that I was ready for whatever came my way. I suppose that is why certain messages were coming and even the images I can assure you I had no control over.

~

Daren was working on Easter Sunday the vision of the scroll was constantly in my view as I did my chores around the house. It was a bizarre experience but I could not switch it off. I knew that was out of my control too. I know I did feel quite tired with it all but wouldn't you if you were reading a book constantly. Even though I was not physically reading it but, on some level, it was in my clear eyes view where ever I looked.

My children watched 'Wizard of Oz' as I went to pick Daren up from work. I sat in the car waiting for Daren to arrive. He had got BBC Radio 2 tuned in and I sat listening to the songs of praise. I suddenly had a flashback of the wizard of oz vision I had 3 months previously and Atlantis. The vision of the scrolls is the information I am receiving. Whatever valid information I need, I am experiencing it now. As I realised this the radio went off for 2 seconds. This was my confirmation that this was happening. At this point I became very emotional and wept with honour and joy. I felt very much loved and protected too at this time. Something is most definitely happening.

When Daren arrived, I just about stopped my tears from flowing and told him that something special is about to happen and is already happening within me. He as usual looked at me and smiled.

~~~Healing~~~

I had driven to my mums to see my Malaysian cousin S who had come to visit England with her brothers. I arrived at my mother's house without any hesitation or getting lost. I thanked the angels for helping me. I was proud to tell S of my experiences of Angels and Ascended Masters. She listened with enthusiasm. She told me how she couldn't wait to read my first book when it was published. I offered her healing. She loved alternative therapies she told me. S and I went to India a couple of years earlier and we visited some Indian temples. I knew she did believe in God and healing. During the healing some important things were revealed, I could sense burning in her stomach also a message for her to forgive past hurts with her mother. She needed to do this. I relayed this message a few times to her. There was also a message that someone was watching over her and I felt it was her great grandmother. During this visit I had also given Paul my sceptic brother-in-law some healing. He was going into hospital for an eye operation and was a little nervous, as any one would be. I felt the healing was good for him. His feedback was that he saw a white light at the end of a tunnel and a feathery figure.

~

The little girl Georgia who lives a few doors away had fallen off her bike whilst playing with my daughter Alysha. Georgia is a gifted sensitive child. I had gone in to her house to see if she was alright. She was bleeding down her left side of her body where she had grazed herself. She was a little traumatised. I instinctively scanned her body and looked into her eyes not knowing why I was doing this. A couple of days later she said she felt calm and fine when she stared into my eyes. She also queried if I was an angel, I chuckled and felt warmth and gratitude although she need not say any more. I felt some other energies were supporting her at that time.

~

As a family we went to the country where we all enjoy the nature and its beauty. But I was too breathless that I struggled to walk the distance. Sometimes I felt that well spiritually that I forgot my body was still quite weak. Daren had to go back to get the car. Nevertheless, we had a lovely picnic that we all enjoyed.

∼◦

I asked the beings of light to help me produce a good book. During the cleansing of my aura, I saw the ॐ aum sign which also means creation of the universe in the Hindu culture.

CHAPTER 4

~~~*The Rabbit*~~~

Alysha had been asking for a pet rabbit recently, I suppose with it being Easter there was more of an obsession. Knowing well that no one would look after it the answer was a no. Well, this particular day she came running into the house claiming she had found a rabbit. We were stunned and went to investigate. There was definitely a rabbit sitting under Daren's car. It was a beautiful hazel colour and was a lop-eared rabbit. Unfortunately, we struggled for a while to figure out whose it could be Alysha became excited thinking, she could acquire it. After knocking on a few neighbours' doors one of the neighbours coaxed it out with some lettuce and took it to the owner and guess what its name was Angel! I think that was Alysha's very short experience of having a rabbit.

~~~*Preparation Is The Key*~~~

I had prepared my space using the aura essence room spray. Jesus Christ was the spray I felt very connected to. This helped to energise the area before I was to do my own healing, it was a good way of clearing vibes that I did not want around me or in the space I was to sit in. Even though I was now working with the public and had not yet recovered, I knew I had to help others. I felt I was guided to give others healing as I had faith that this was my path. I would recover one day whenever that would be. My goal was not to sit with the feeling of being helpless but rather to journey along and try to continue life as normal as possible. Going into my healing I felt the sereneness and the ability that I could bring calm into my whole being. In the healing the pale colours washed my view. I was definitely in touch with the angels as I could feel a feathery sensation around me. I could see a big polar bear in my view. The message that came was I needed to rest because my spiritual journey was going to be an adventure releasing some more of my hidden gifts. This made sense as I had fatigue and I just needed to listen to this message. I was once again told not to be outrun by the hounds as I could clearly see a fox and the racoon was implying that I needed to watch out for someone who had alterior motives with me. As I finished off the healing I fell asleep, I knew that this feathery being was enveloping me because it was so obviously felt. It actually made me feel very protected and special. I know now that trust was all that was needed. I woke up feeling well but above all I saw an owl, it was brown with a distinct pattern on it. Its whole wingspan was huge. It appeared to show me that I should fly. The message was that sharing and cooperation is healthier rather than competition. This was of course very interesting as I was to present an Angel Evening at a public venue in my local area. The idea was to share what I know and to welcome many others on board. To welcome them to what I have experienced and to give them knowledge of angel healing as it is the newest form of healing available to humanity. This was about awakening our true selves, awakening to the power of love through angels.

Again, my angel card readings were telling me that my feelings will be my guide as I progress in life after all these are the gifts of the Divine, and I was to open my arms to receive all that is to come my way. My life was being reviewed not only by me but from them upstairs. My first book was being written as I was guided to do so. Even though I never dreamt of producing a book and so quickly. My heart was full of joy knowing that positive outcomes were waiting for me. Everything is only a matter of time. Be patient. Be patient. My very special messages were received with gratitude. The feathery sensation had now lasted with me for two days. I continuously tried to brush this feeling off my face and yet nothing on the physical level was there. I couldn't wait to tell Lyn, my friend that this was what I had been feeling.

∽

My Angel Evening had arrived and Lyn was supporting me. My intuition was to take the extension cable. I had ignored my own guidance. The venues cable did not work so I telephoned my husband to bring the cable to me. It just goes to show that we should listen and trust our own intuition in the first place even if it is something simple. The evening was busy at this venue. But the evening itself was important as there were connections to be made. The opportunity had arisen for this event and I did trust that it would be fine. I had managed to keep to a flow. At times spirits were disturbing me and I had to backtrack what I was saying. I felt that there were some people who had not let go of their deceased loved ones and that was my distraction that evening. I was aware of this as I was familiar of this happening before. My stammering and stuttering were more frequent than usual. I obviously tried not to let it take over the evening as I had more information to share. Even though I received overall good feedback for the evening, I was over confident about the angel healings but also realised that sometimes people want a cure and this is not the case for every individual as Lyn made this apparent to me. A healing takes place just at the level they need to receive. A person can be healed but also changes may need to take place for the recipient. Sometimes it is not a need for a rescue for the time being but a change of circumstances or a review of how one decides to cope with life. Even those terminally ill who receive healing will pass over healed. Those that wanted card readings received them. For some it was an emotional time, I knew that this was realisation and a healing time for them. That very night I had constant contact from spirits who had passed over. I felt my intuition was correct to whom the spirits were trying to connect with, but when contacting these people, they were not interested in releasing the spirit to the other side properly. They, themselves felt this was a comfort to them. But is that a good idea? I have received guidance from the angels that the spirits should be released. Even more so the spirits themselves want to be released so that they can journey on the other side. Not everyone though can understand this.

~

Si, the interesting gentleman who has lived an exciting life full of many experiences, felt he has received luck and synchronicities. He would say he was in the right place at the right time. His journey on the spiritual path was quite easy but wanted to learn more and wanted to advance his journey. Now he was all set for more angel healings. The previous session he received guidance. This time he received healing for doubts and fears held in his energy centres. It was indeed an intense session as coming out of the healing we both felt the affects.

~~~*Learning Something New*~~~

I had now booked to do the aura essences course but I previously doubted I needed to do it. I was quite content with the angel healing course.

Will I Am, my aura essences teacher welcomed all the students with a hug and a kiss on the cheek. By now I had already built up a good customer relationship as I ordered all my products from him. Again, meeting the other students on the course was interesting as we all have our own journeys that we have travelled along. During the course of the day, I was receiving confirmation from the Archangels and their connection with aura essences. I even felt a down pouring of energies from them. As I still had not recovered from the fibromyalgia and the chronic fatigue, I was quite exhausted. Anubis the Egyptian Guard Dog, seemed to have had a strong link with me as I shared this with Will I Am.

~~

Back at the clinic, new clients were coming for the angel healings, some were therapists. I had received great guidance from Kuthumi, an ascended master that people are out there trying to chase the energies of Divine, travelling from one country to another. 'Be still and just feel it' was the message. When the time is right for each individual then you will receive what you have been looking for. You cannot force the force.

This same evening, I asked God what was next for me. My vision came of a male and female. There was an intense light shining from within them. I was told to see the shining light in all and to help this light to grow. Every time I had received Divine guidance, I would feel overwhelmed with pure love and joy. This was my true-life purpose; my experiences were showing me the way.

Even those who were the average ordinary person, without being stereotypical of spiritual and non spiritual people, would be astonished to find how I had received information of their imbalances in their bodies.

~

Days of using the aura essence products I could see those distinct colours as I closed my eyes in bed. During this same night my vision came through in full colour of a courtroom. It was an empty court room but the words that read underneath were 'No obligation.' There were two meanings for me with this message. The first was that I was warned not to make any major mistakes. Secondly, that I could be speaking out in a formal situation but, under 'No obligation.' I had also received some sacred esoteric spiritual mandalas.

~~~*Specialists Appointment*~~~

The next day I had noticed how the magpies and many other garden birds had returned back into my garden those that I had not seen for a few weeks. I was so relieved to see them and the magic that they brought back with them. I had contacted a couple of the people that I felt I needed to guide to let go of their deceased love ones, but I also felt that they were not ready to do so. I felt as though I was in an awkward position but hey, I felt I had to at least make these people aware. That very night my vision showed a tap and a person. The message that came with it was 'To let it flow out from a person.' Who this person was, I did not know at the time? Another night on the run I received more esoteric shapes.

My appointment with my specialist had arrived and he checked my lungs and looked through my file. He said he was pleased with my recovery. But also knew that my complete recovery would take some time. He told me to be careful with the fibromyalgia and chronic fatigue and to go up the slower slope rather than trying to make a full recovery too quick. I felt he was aware of my personality type, but I also felt he was wrong as my inner self was telling me it would be fine. I was more optimistic than him even though he showed his caring personality.

I am aware there was a blockage in my air waves as I could not breathe without pain on every breath.

This was my moment to tell him that I was working just a few hours a week as an angel healing practitioner. I told him quite firmly that something had happened to me the previous year and that doctors would not understand this but people like him should listen to people like me. He instantly put his pen on the table sat back in his chair and held both hands together at his solar plexus. I felt something special was with me at this time as I spoke. I told him that whether people are religious or not they should listen to what has to be said. I told him this is what happened to me when the angels came into my life and now, I am a healer working from a clinic. He noted this and wished me luck in the future. This evidently was also the day he discharged me. This was absolutely fine with me as I felt the hospital was doing their duty to keep a check on me so that I would have a steady progress. But ultimately all the recovery was down to alternative therapies.

In some sense we look for security from medical staff with medical support when we do not know what is causing illness. This had served its purpose with me.

CHAPTER 5

~~~Business Of Commerce~~~

I had a telephone call months ago from my local business of commerce to ask me to become a member. I decided to join this chamber. What did I have to lose? I felt it was good to do this for some reason. I attended the networking lunch. I realised once there that I was a very unusual candidate for this meeting. Most people were lawyers, bankers, big corporate and local businesses. I was very confident attending a big networking group such as this. Yes, I would say a little out of my depth as I am not a harsh business woman. I managed to give out my leaflets and quite happily chatted to other members. I had an extremely calm feeling about me. There was no room for fear. I felt quite at ease making new contacts. I even met someone who was interested in me working from their centre. At this moment I did turn the person down as I had previously wanted to work from that centre but was turned away. I just needed time to settle for now. I was certain that If my energy needed to take a u turn I would. But not yet. This particular day my cards were telling me to consult an expert and to dream big. I felt extremely happy to the point of having those joyful tears that I had been experiencing over the last year.

❧

I had an interesting night out with girls from my new place of work. I had not been out for some time and in some sense was not really bothered about being out as I was quite content with what I had in life. My health was of utmost importance. During the evening I was feeling the injuries and back pain of other girls. I did relay this information to them. I actually felt very calm and serene. Another of the girls also did a therapy and felt that I probably needed healing. I did in the long run but not this day as I was so content.

~~~Ascended Masters~~~

The following day I had been on a course with Lyn and received a lovely connection with the ascended masters. With it being the summer months Daren had wanted to go to the beer garden by the canal. I felt the aura of a lady quite largely behind me. As we bought our drinks, we sat next to one another, I instinctively knew she was a therapist. The colours she wore very vibrant with beautiful crystal jewellery. She made it very aware to me that there was to be a mind, body spirit fair on at our local civic hall. I did listen to her but I knew I could not attend it. This lady only was with us for half an hour but she talked non stop. It was actually a reflection of me. How bizarre. I wanted to give her my business card but she left as quickly as she came. Even Daren picked up that her vibes were strange. We were left wondering who this lady was just imparting information.

Lyn had arrived to take me for my aura essences course which was with Will I Am. My cards were telling me that I have to learn something to be able to teach it. I was quite open minded with the guidance. So, we shall have to see what exactly I need to teach. I had no further plans with this particular course.

Daren had told me that three people he knew and worked with had passed away in the same week. I relayed this information to Lyn she reminded me to say a prayer and take them to the light. Yes, I had forgotten why Daren was making it clear to me over and over again. It was simply as Lyn said to take them to the light, it was an indirect request. You see it was quite easy for me to forget this task as I was now becoming busy with all the new things I needed to learn.

~

This particular day I had a beautiful connection with master Kuthumi the master of links with the angels and humans on earth. I was unaware I was wearing this particular ascended master's colours. I felt very happy as the joy was over spilling from my inner self. To the point towards tears of joy.

My two clients came for healing, for both of them I gave a soul therapy massage. My first client had recognised on a soul level that at conception there was a purpose and link for her life. On many levels it was not clear to her why she became emotional but there was a soul emotional trigger. On a mental subconscious level, she knew what her life was about. The other lady was indeed stuck in her own life as she could not see beyond materialism. I sensed her distress in life and the resentment she carried to every level of her body system. She was still clinging on to the victim that she once was. But from my own experience of life that is not the healthy option towards freedom of the soul. Once caught up in the poor me scenario you are creating a victim situation, never ready to move on. She held on to the divorce from many years ago, the nuclear family separation, which is also known as a broken household. The lady was still going to be the victim in the future. I explained how she really needed to move on from this as it was the cause of her cancer which was at that moment in remission. To some extent this lady understood this but said she had tried other therapies to overcome the depth of her depressive way of thinking. She enjoyed her session of healing and left calmer and even something to think about.

That very night I was awoken to be shown a beautiful green background and in front stood a man wearing a cloak. He just stood there looking at me. I felt the message that was non verbal came from the master Hilarion. The master was telling me that I had shown them the way. The deeper understanding for me was the link with this master through the aura essences system. I was actually studying it but did not know who this master was until much later. It all made sense to me eventually. In the early hours of the morning in half asleep mode, I saw cuboids. I was somewhere there, with the shapes. It was interesting like some other dimension.

I had prepared myself for working a few hours a day also taking into account that I needed to rest properly as I had not recovered from my condition.

The next day I had not planned to do much. I was meditating and out of no where I was shown a convertible car. It was not as though I was in control of what was going to be shown to me it was them. They were guiding me. Sometimes the images were clear and then at times fleeting. It was a beautiful vehicle and I know that I am not knowledgeable about technology or quality of vehicles and materialistically wanting the best. It was not in my character to want branded items well definitely not just lately. I was content in more than one way. That was finding spirituality. Unfortunately, though this particular day I felt very ill as I could not breathe. I stayed in bed for the rest of the day. I was not angry with anyone. I just had to allow this condition to pass. I knew of some people who had suffered for years with chronic fatigue, but I knew one day I would recover, just sit tight.

⁓

The next day I had visions of a racoon and a fox. The messages were clear as I knew that I could achieve that which needed achieving. At this time, I was also given the name Djwhal Khul.

Djwhal khul was the youngest of ascended masters to leave the physical world after completing his duty on earth. He was the healing ray for the angel healing system. I felt I was told invoke this master for my healing. I had not long got up this morning and felt I needed to rest more in bed as the breathlessness and fatigue was all too much. I was only too aware for when the children were to come home that I was to manoeuvre gently as not to waste too much energy whilst seeing to them.

I took my time as I prepared my self for the day. I used my aura essence equilibrium bottle to assist me, I needed the extra support as I was at the clinic. A therapist had come for a healing. She asked if any messages came for her after the session. There was a message it was all about happiness. As we spoke about her grandparents on the other side a picture of the ascended master Lady Portia flew of the window ledge. It was almost as if it was in slow motion, I watched it fly off the windowsill from behind her. I was amazed. I also know that a lot of people who were coming to see me had a sad loss in the family and the clients were always drawn to Lady Portia. This lady's grandparents wanted to be sent to the light. The significant image to me was about transferring souls to the light. Anubis was the undertaker of souls to the light. I had my own understanding as this had happened on a number of occasions. After this instant soul transferring of the grandparents had happened, the further messages from the angel card reading were that she has the tools to work at a balanced level and she was to have a fun filled life too. This made a lot of sense for this lady as she left with a smile.

~

My friend Alison had her healing and as she relaxed in her conservatory, I could see there was a golden sword. Instantly the message of sword in the stone had appeared, it was King Arthur's. I felt Alison had a life time in the Arthurian times. Alison had most definitely had throat issues in her past life as that was what I was picking up. Even in this life time she had held herself back from speaking of how she truly felt. I did express to her that she should make her voice to be heard too, she should express how she felt about things. A couple of hours later she contacted me to say thank you and that she felt very happy. I had noticed how speaking to others generally about what I could do to assist them made them tearful. The truth of the matter was that I believed I could do it.

~~~*Angel Evening*~~~

I had prepared my messages for my angel evening. Everyone arrived to a cosy home from home atmosphere. The gentle music playing in the background and burning aromas of essential incense sticks made the evening a relaxing special event.

The burning of the incense sticks is what I had been used to all my life as my mother regularly burned them. To be truthful so was the music a must, whilst doing her prayer and cleansing ritual. It is quite funny as I was growing up, I did understand this ritual but did not appreciate it and now here I am following a similar tradition but to my belief. At the end of the day, we are all one, we are all learning to do the same but in different belief systems.

The evening had begun and everyone listened with enthusiasm. As I asked the audience about their experiences one lady commented on my inner strength and wept. I knew she was receiving healing, healing for her own weaknesses. The strength was something she really needed in her life right then so listening to my story touched her soul. I walked over to her side and hugged her and sat with her for a while. Her anxiety and nervousness were entering my body. We all discussed angels and experiences, by now everyone was relaxed. The meditation was powerful. Archangel Sandalphon grounded everyone and Archangel Michael protected all those present. Many in the room once again felt the brushing sensation on their legs and were deeply relaxed. One person was a previous client and thought during the healing sessions she felt a pair of hands on her chest and when she opened her eyes my hands were not near that particular area. I explained that the angels were always around giving the healing. The audience left happy and uplifted. The lady that was upset literally left skipping saying how happy she was. The young couple had a change in breathing during the meditation but this was quite normal as some stuck energy was being removed from them. The young man had found it difficult to look into my eyes and even Alysha's my daughters earlier that evening. He could not understand why. The messages were a link to every person's life as they explained. It was a successful evening thanks to the Angels and Archangels.

~~~*Trauma*~~~

The healing was now reaching heights of beautiful experiences for some people as they were receiving messages via the healing sessions. Others felt relaxed and felt the healing was benefiting them.

Lyn my friend had come for healing she required healing for her solar plexus and heart centre. This removal of debris was cleared via my hands. Her throat was the core of her problem she had past life traumas linked to her throat. Lyn had felt the healing had worked to a deep level, she remarked it was the best healing she had ever received. Again, the angels are the tool for the fabulous results.

The past few nights I had dreams of Daren dying. I was crying traumatised in my dream but also woke up in reality crying. As I astral travel a lot, I had been out to another plane. There too I sobbed. I woke up needing to find some tissues in the bathroom. I felt I had shed many tears. I also saw a coffin it most definitely was connecting to death. I was traumatised by my dreams and the astral travelling to a destination to see a coffin and death.

CHAPTER 6

~~~*My Beloved*~~~

The following morning, I woke up breathless. I was to attend a workshop facilitated by Moyra, who is a spiritual author. I was indeed requiring extra angelic support as I was to drive to her house and see the whole day through. The angels surely were not going to let me down. As I arrived at Moyra's workshop I met other people. I was feeling fragile so I tired not to waste too much energy. Throughout the workshop I was receiving confirmations of my thoughts. The amazing meditation took us to meet our beloved behind one of the doors. We may see our beloved in many ways. I am sure some of the people would see the beloved as a husband or wife, even children or deceased loved ones. For me I knew who this beloved was. As we came closer to finding out who this person was my heart started to beat faster and faster. At one stage my heart was beating that loud that I thought it was going to pop out of my chest. My physical body was experiencing something great but my emotional, mental and spiritual bodies were in contact with what I would say is heaven. I had not experienced this before. My excitement could not withhold me. As Moyra guided us my heart was uncontrollable, the thudding in my heart was exceptionally loud as I put my hand on my heart centre to calm myself. In the meditation I approached the big wooden door that had wrought iron fixtures. As I opened the door, I saw Jesus Christ standing in the back of a medieval room. He was shrouded with the shadow of the room. Yet there he stood just looking. I wanted to cry. I wanted to smile. I wanted to laugh and shout to everyone that Jesus was my beloved. I was 100% delighted and honoured that my beloved was Jesus Christ. This person could have been anyone. For me it was Jesus. My heart accelerated with joy beyond anything I had experienced on the physical plane. Wow!!!!!!!!!!!!!!!!!!!!!!!!!!!!!!!

For the rest of that day, I was elated. I had also spoken to Caroline and Lyn my colleagues they said it was Jesus for them too.

What an honour it was for all three of us. Lyn had spoken out giving some words of wisdom which were spoken extremely well. For some reason I was very proud of her.

~~~Trust The Transformation~~~

As the days led into May, I could feel symptoms of my client's hours before they came to see me. They certainly were not my symptoms. I noticed how I was becoming more and more sensitive. My clients were suffering from severe anxiety and it overwhelmed my body as I felt a little faint. One of the ladies expressed how she felt happiness had increased with the assistance of angel healings. One gentleman, this specific day remarked how his well-being had an uplifting effect on him. I became quite emotional for I was actually hearing all these beautiful comments from my clients. You see I do not need to convince my readers of the effects of how healing has worked on these souls they are their own voice. I was able to remove other people's energy from my own, the angels helped me with this as I was now seeing more people.

Asleep after a good day healing, I received a message in the middle of the night. The message I would like to say came from the angels, a gentle female spoke to me, "Djwhal Khul had channelled through Alice Bailey, now Djwhal Khul is channelling through others to bring light to souls." I was given this message a couple of times in the night. In fact, I woke up remembering word for word the whole message. I knew I had an important connection with this master over the eleven months, as I was seeing him regularly. The next day I was shown a white dove in flight, yes, much peace is essential to all of us for our well-being. I was confident I could do my duty as a healer as long as I look after myself.

One of my client's Sarah asked for her crystals to be cleansed with the angelic vibration as she was needing the support from them as she was to journey through her transformations. She was in the eye of the storm. She thanked me for the continuous support, I was only too happy to give her guidance. Sitting in my kitchen talking to her I could feel her emotions as I was beginning to well up.

I was still reading my cards and I was told to complete a project; this was my first book. I was also told that it would be ok.

One of my dreams would be to open a healing clinic. As I was out with my eldest daughter, I felt I could do this with the help of my family members. I would love for this dream to come to fruition. I continued having horrific dreams of family members dying and drowning, friends dumping their rubbish on me and the elderly. I was at this time using Pallas Athena quintessence and wondered if it was enhancing my dreaming.

My cards were telling me it was a time for creativity and transformation, peace and tranquillity with the trees and forests. Monday was the day for all this to happen. This actually connected with our holiday to Scotland a week on Monday to the forest. This was my time to take time out to transform my inner self on a deeper level.

For the last two days I had not been too well. A little girl had gone missing on holiday and it was on the news and in every paper. Sharon was my eldest and she had recently been going out and had not let us known of her whereabouts. I was now beside myself with worry as I could not contact her. My daughter did arrive home eventually. However, my point is that I could empathise with the family who had lost their little girl. I felt as though I was going through the motions with them. My body was going through a shock and tried to shut down just like months previously when I was paralysed. I had to ask the angels to help me to be well as I had clients at the clinic. I had prepared my self for the day but I was very exhausted. When I got to the clinic there was no electricity. This had now happened two weeks on the run. I started to pray to the angels and miraculously it came on. I thanked the angels.

I found it very strange as I was meditating, I received the missing girls' name. There was no other information but her name. What was the link here? I had no idea what the angels were trying to tell me.

As now I was becoming more established with clients wanting angel healings. I did what I could in whatever time I could. I was aware of my body too, I needed healing everyday too. I made it aware to my family that I was recovering but there were some times when I felt so very ill. My body was becoming stronger but with time. As I was helping people and I was receiving messages for myself too. I could see a white bird in flight. This was showing me I could do what I was doing, it is through help from spirit. I can work from the clinic I set up from, just one healing every now and then will be fine, if the angels bring more clients then I will be able to do more. Sally one of my clients arrived for her healing and found the healing to be amazing as she felt so relaxed.

I had done my angel cards and they were telling me to complete a project. I knew this linked with my first book Seeing is Believing, Believing is Seeing. I was told everything was OK. These words I had been given so many times. I was also being told to be creative and transformations are waiting for me. There will be peace and tranquillity go in to the woods, transform the inner self. Well, this made sense as we were due to go to Scotland into forest.

~~~Family Healing~~~

On 25th June in the night, I kept seeing a female wearing a modern striped top. Who was this female? That very morning at about 4.30 I received a message that my cousin S had passed away. I could not believe the message. I telephoned my aunt straight away, soon it was confirmed she passed away an hour ago in Malaysia, my legs gave way beneath me again it was my body trying to shut down. I could not cope with the trauma. My heart rate changed as I lay sobbing in my bed. It was disbelief, we had only seen her months previously as she did her tour of Britain. That was the day of mourning for most of the family. I continued to go into the clinic for healing. My clients had not noticed a thing. My strength was to continue with a couple of hours at the clinic. My mourning with the family took place later. I knew there was more to this story as I endeavoured to find out, a couple of days passed and I managed to get to the truth. It was a horrific dealing. But my heart and the angels would not lie to me. When I tried to tell Daren of my findings my heart rate quickened almost in anxiety state and then my voice changed as I spoke to him. My intuition was telling me it was S speaking. It was just like I knew it. I was aware of this kind of feeling from when other souls have tried to contact me. This was deadly serious it was not out of a movie. I found out she had been poisoned. Somehow, I was searching on the internet and I found a dark website that celebrated her death, it was a complete shock. I don't know why but I became scared myself. I was told that during her dying she knew she had been poisoned. Her uncle was with her all the way to the end of life. My uncle told me, as we kept in touch during this time that she requested one thing, it was fresh water melon. My uncle said he helped her to get the water from the melon and she was weak. It was her favourite fruit. After this phone call it left a deep impression of sadness and how could this even happen. So very sad, she passed away days before her 30th birthday.

～⌒

As a few days had passed I had now received images of a bungalow, a pair of glasses and scissors. At this moment I did not look at this message in great detail but please read on as this message is quite significant for my future.

As I was a qualified teacher of angel healings, I had a list of people already displaying interest in this down pouring of light from the Angelic Kingdom. My first course had arrived and I had my very first small group. Sharon my daughter was one of the students. As soon as we started, I felt a warm glow of the angelic energy surround me. Sharon was definitely crying inside during the attunement. On the exterior she seemed fine but I knew that internally she was weeping. After the course she admitted she was. I knew that this was a profound course for all students present. This would undoubtedly have touched them to the very core of their soul.

Alysha was not very well and I was feeling every bit of her illness. The only way we would both feel well was if I could heal her. El Moyra the Master of Divine Will was present and so were the nature spirits. When she was well, I became well.

Now that Sharon was trained in the healing levels one and two, she could practise healing on me. She had followed the method perfectly. I had felt the heaviness on my chest as my chronic fatigue had not gone yet. I had pain in my back as well as my lower limbs. The healing was good because after five minutes the pain and heaviness in my chest had left me. The colours in my minds eye were fantastic, the pale shades of pink, the peaceful tranquil environment. Sharon started to close down the healing. I sensed she had become tearful. Her feedback confirmed mine. She told me she could see a pure white horse and I was sitting on it. I was in fact in full flow riding this pure white horse. She saw the horse stand upright as I was still on it. It was a triumphant stage. Sharon described it so passionately it was great since she does not quite see and sense as much as my other two children. Sharon had continued telling me that a female had approached her and that she seemed very much real and in the physical body. Sharon described this female as having straight hair with long strands of a fringe to the side of her face. Sharon could only see half of her brown skinned face smiling at her. The face came closer in view before fading into the distance. Sharon called her back asking who she was. Sharon wanted confirmation of this female, although knowing this had to be her. Sharon became emotional. Her identity was confirmed to her. Amazed at what she saw and the closeness this person appeared at made a deep impact on Sharon. Discussing the whole scenario was emotional for mother and daughter. This was my cousin S who had very recently passed over. I knew she was alright as she came to show herself from the spirit world.

As we walked out of the healing space, I received another message from Lady Portia about bringing justice and allowing my heart to become balanced. Anubis had also brought me a message of allowing this soul to pass to the other world.

Sharon was now practising on Tristen as he wanted to receive healing. As they were doing that, I needed to tell my mum about S being in the right place and that she was fine. As I started to talk to mum, I saw S's feet and she was wearing a pink sari. My mum understood some aspects of this, by now she understood the work that I was doing and knew that people from the spirit world could make contact. During my conversation with mum Sharon came running to find me to explain what happened in Tristen's session. Tristen followed Sharon into the room and started describing the significant details of his healing session. He went on to say that he saw a light at the end of a tunnel, in the light stood a person. His eyes filled with tears. I asked him who he thought this person was. He immediately said it was my cousin S. He was being brave not to shed the tears from his eyes. Sharon stood silently by her brother's side as he spoke. I called him over and asked if he was alright. As he sat himself down next to me, he smiled sorrowfully. I explained to him that it was good to show emotions and as a family we were available to listen to him if he needed to talk. This was undoubtedly a powerful experience for him. Sharon and I had not mentioned to Daren or my other two children of my healing session, so this was Tristen's own experience of a family member who had passed away. Bearing in mind he is only a thirteen-year-old boy. Not by any means a first experience for him with spirits and souls, however still a touching and sad experience for him as he had only met S months previously. As Tristen made his way for a restful evening Sharon said he had not disclosed a name to her but had cried in the healing session. Sharon was feeling the same emotions in Tristen's session as with mine. Sharon went on to say there was a definite presence in the room too. Sharon, to some extent felt sense of uncomfortableness. I reassured her she was in control of doing what needs to be done.

~~~*Friends Healing*~~~

As time was progressing, I was now in awe of angel healings and felt very compassionate about taking this further to the general public. I explored other avenues of taking it to professional organisations and centres. I felt very much that this is where I need to be heading, I had meetings and chatted on the phone to explain what the benefits could be for many people. Some healthcare professions unfortunately did not take this system seriously. I was even trying to explain how much I was benefiting from the angel healings myself. Some church organisations I had chatted to did not want to even understand how one can bring balance to the mind body and soul. I understood that their religion was putting a barrier to that which could bring harmony for one another and the planet. Is it their ego that is restricting them to open up to a whole new world of possibilities? Are we not in those times now that we need to merge our thoughts and minds to bring equilibrium? To also bring in higher consciousness as that is ultimately what humanity is evolving towards. At times my heart sank as I felt the ego of certain religions was forbidding a unified existence. What is all this partitioned practising? Are we not all one? We came from the same creator irrespective to colour or creed, culture or religion.

In July 2007, I had meditated for mother earth. The one-hour healing meditation was revealing a foetus. For the last 5 minutes I received an extremely powerful vibration. I was told that mother earth was now being re-birthed. It was a content healing meditation.

～

Again, those receiving healing were feeling satisfied in life. The messages were affirming that I was being protected. The time I received this message was 3.33, of course it was the Divine number of truths. I trusted this message.

～

On meeting my angel healing colleagues who were now my dear friends, we chatted about how our lives were progressing. Lyn had started lunch for us. Caroline declined the offer of having healing. I always thought it was a good idea to give one another a healing session as an exchange as we all need healing. To receive shows appreciation for one's soul as well as self love and acceptance. Sometimes we give to others and forget about ourselves especially doing the work we do when nurturing others. So, to accept something from another as a gift is good for the soul too.

Caroline had started healing me, instantly I felt her healing angel surround me. I felt the warmth and love. Throughout the session I felt my diaphragm tighten to the point of not being able to take deep breaths. The sharp pain on the left side of my chest commenced secondary down to my left leg. I just allowed this to continue as I was aware that I was safe and it was a matter of letting go of something that I had held on to. My third eye stimulated a vibration that swirled as my palm chakras were activated with the same vibration. Caroline gave me feedback of my session which also gave insight into the Egyptian era and a golden pyramid that was held above my crown chakra, she also saw one of the aura essences bottles. The aura essence bottle was the one that would be applied to the diaphragm that was totally ideal. The visions of the animals, panda and bear also told me of strength, balance, confidence, healing and grounding.

Caroline was a fantastic healer and very accurate with the feedback that was given. She always amazed me. I knew which aspects of that healing were poignant, the parts of my past that still needed healing.

We often think that we are healed from one session but some may require more than one as we have many levels to heal anyway.

For me initially it is about feeling the energy of the angelic realms that is always overwhelming. It is an honour to be that light energy.

We had made our way downstairs as Lyn had now prepared our lunch. Caroline had to remind me many times during this lunch to breathe as I spoke so fast. Caroline's wide brown eyes looked in amazement as I spoke so speedily before we all fell into fits of laughter. We laughed until our stomachs were in pain.

My cards were telling me that my loved ones who had passed over were now looking over me. That was very reassuring, especially due to the death of my cousin. I was asked also to have courage with those things that I want to pursue and to be more in awareness of feminine leadership role which very much linked to the aura essence bottle that I was guided by Caroline to use.

~

Parveen Smith

The Moseley family were going through an ordeal of harassment which had escalated as a problem. I felt impelled to help them. I had received a vision in the night of white doves then I could see unpleasant faces but I could also see a dot of white light in these unpleasant faces. I lay there wondering why I was shown this image. After the realisation I decided to send healing and light and protection to the Moseley household. I realised why I was guided to send pure light and protection to this family as they were living in fear. I was guided to send pure light and unconditional love to those harassing the family.

CHAPTER 7

~~~*Taking My Self Further*~~~

I had this drive and inspiration to help as many people as possible and spreading the word of healing modalities such as what I had learned. I had meditated and I was guided to ring the fire station and present a small talk on healing therapies and how it could help those who bring service through their brave actions. I had immediately written a brief letter of what I wanted to present and personally delivered the letter. They invited me to give my talk. I was then also invited to give the same talk to all watches on site. This was very exciting for me as I knew that the angels were guiding me to be in certain places. I had also become a member of my local business of commerce. At first, I wondered why I needed to be there. Why even waste my money to become a member, as what I did was not quite what the business world would understand? At this point it did not marry up. After attending a couple of the chambers networking meetings, I felt proud that I was actually spreading the word of angel healings. It was very inspiring as I looked back at each event and smiled at myself. I may not have gained any business but on some level, I felt I was doing my job. Others may think that I may have attended this sort of event out of naivety or stupidity but I didn't care what others thought as I was spreading the word of healings, an alternative complementary therapy with a holistic approach. I had been in the right place to even pass messages on. Some needed to hear that financial gain would not necessarily bring them happiness. Some needed to hear that they needed to bring balance in their lives. I was a channel after all allowing others to hear what they needed to.

~~~*Visions*~~~

I had a vision of entering a church. Where the church was or to which sector it belonged to, I was not sure. I could see the bell at the top of the building swinging slowly. Shortly afterwards I saw Paul the Venetian. What was he trying to tell me? Then St Germain appeared showing his great presence. At this point I was extremely pleased as I had not seen the great master of transformation and healing. I felt the glow amidst the dark night lying in my bed. I was honoured. I found out that Paul the Venetian was the master of Divine love of the third ray, he assists in the path of love and compassion, patience and understanding.

As I had already said that I was in the right place at the right time to give messages I had approached certain businesses to receive this amazing healing modality. One particular lady telephoned me after the feedback I had given her. She felt I was correct in telling her there was something missing from her life. I also explained how important it was for her to have some training for her own career. She also agreed. She had arranged to see me. Yes, the angels were working with me and took me to this lady.

I had been suffering with flu like symptoms over the last three days, maybe this was still my body not fully recovered and the stress of losing a family member.

Caroline had arrived to give me some transpersonal counselling. This was my second session and Caroline sensed this was something I would benefit from due to my previous healing session with her. When I reached a place within this session, I was told that everything was alright. I needed to have time out and plenty of rest. I welcomed that as I had not recovered from fibromyalgia and chronic fatigue. My body was relaying messages as I was lacking in energy sometimes, I felt energised but I also needed plenty of rest to recover from any activity I undertook.

I meditated and self-healed as this was my tool to recovery. It was just a matter of time I told myself that I would be free from this restraining condition. It was 4.00am during this particular time I was shown Alice Bailey's name and Djwal Khul's name. I could see the rules within the angel healing manual. Shortly afterwards I could see a consultant wearing a pure white gown, cap and face mask just like surgeons would do when operating. Was this telling me that I was to approach a hospital next, what was this message telling me?

～

I had now received my first published copy of Seeing Is Believing, Believing Is Seeing and I was holding it in my hands. It was a euphoric feeling. A moment of accepting that this was something I never dreamt of holding in my very own hands in this lifetime. But I was. I even asked the postman to stay a few minutes whilst I opened the package, he could see how excited I was. As I showed him my book he smiled and said well done. I started to phone my family and friends with such excitement my book had arrived.

～

This evening I had a vision of soldiers from war times wearing green uniforms and helmets. I have never been one for history and therefore can't describe exactly what era this may have been from, possibly 1945 to modern day. The soldiers were walking but I could also see some sitting too. They were sent to an occasion and that was all I was told. I was also shown a spade a dark place which also looked like a cemetery above I was shown a white cross. At this point I did not know when this was for.

It was just only a week or so later that I got a letter from An Army Presentation Team. The invitation was to update us on recent changes in the army and how they interact with sections of society.

It was now the last few days of September 2007. The summer weather was coming to a close and I felt quite positive with life. I was now fulfilling fundamental parts of my purpose. This event was by invitation only. It was an honour to be at the event to hear how the army worked in society.

～

My vision in the night showed me the words 'entrepreneur evening' on a piece of paper also on it was the word 'weekend'. Now I had no idea what this was leading to. During this same evening I sensed my body going into a deep sense of relaxation almost like a deep sleep but I was to some extent aware that I was astral travelling. I went to India during this astral travel where I know there was a lot of unfinished business. I was aware that the people I was seeing had all grown up. This was a necessary part of my spiritual journey in the now moment. I had to put things to rest and I felt that this astral travelling did just that for me. It was for sure a strange experience but worthwhile as I did not need to carry karma any more my own journey excelled and was speedy and I did not need any barriers or restrictions from the past holding me back.

The next evening the same words 'entrepreneur evening' and 'weekend' were shown to me. I could see there were more words followed on a document and managed to read 'food.' This will make more sense a little later.

~~~*Lessons To Be Learned*~~~

I had followed on to do more courses within the aura essence system. I had met someone who promised to do something in return as an exchange but never fulfilled their part of the bargain. I felt used. I had already sensed a negative vibe and felt uneased by the scenario I had put myself in. To some extent the other person was an overpowering individual. I suppose this was still an area I needed to become assertive in. I believed I was destined to meet this person it was to teach me something. But I did not listen to my true feelings and went along with an exchange that I thought could have worked. I had a sleepless part of the night. I even had pain in my chest and a nervous feeling about this. I wanted to decline the offer but couldn't do it.

~

Another situation followed this one which also gave me warning signs as I was driving to a venue to do a talk. Something was not going to go as well as I thought. I was very much judged and criticised at the event. I asked for the angels to support me, I was brave not to have stood and cried as I was made to feel worthless. I defended my cause and stood up to my beliefs. The audience in the room became judgemental some agreed with my view's others did not. As I was ready to leave the venue, I was very much challenged by the same person who criticised me. At that same moment four people stood and surrounded me as though they were protecting me from this one individual verbally attacking me. I felt so much spiritual support at this moment that these people did not realise what they were doing, it helped me as if they were my four guardians. I felt reassured that it was all OK. Even though I left the building emotional I also knew I did a dutiful job. I was not getting paid for this I was working very much on a spiritual level awakening others to a new way of understanding. I had to learn that some will accept what I felt I was guided to say and some would not. I was not doing this to offend anyone. I could in one sense quite easily walk away from doing this spiritual work just on the fact alone I was made to feel worthless or even degraded. But I decided to continue.

That very night I saw a wolf and a tree. The wolf was telling me that I was a spiritual teacher. The tree was all about grounding my knowledge and keeping me grounded. I also saw a pyramid and a phoenix. The pyramid was telling me it is an extremely mighty symbol. At the physical level it is a building, showing regeneration, and in spiritual regard the pyramid is the guardian of the power. The pyramid is a fluent energy which penetrates the material foundation with the spiritual regions. Angels also links with the pyramid shapes.

My cards were telling me to look after myself and that there were things that could come to fruition. I was told to focus on my strengths which I was always clear about. Even thought the reminder every now and again was giving me strength.

~

My vision a few days later came through of a house in Bulgaria. I could see a tap dripping at the kitchen sink there was also an ironing board. My brother-in-law had a share holiday home in Bulgaria I wonder if this was about that.

~

I was also reminded to ring a spiritual healer whom I had not seen or spoken to in a while. I think I needed to clear a few issues with him. I was told 'do not throw your pearls to the swine's'. What this meant was if something is valuable to you others may not see its value and you could be wasting your time and effort.

⁓

I had now met old colleagues I had not spoke to in a while and they queried about what job I was doing at this moment. Talking to others about this was exciting as they too found what I was saying interesting. The interest was gathering for my first book.

⁓

I approached more organisations for talks. Many men were interested in the subject matter of healing. They were amazed to see how colour could reflect their lives. What a pleasant experience it was for everyone.

⁓

Lao Tsu and Quan Yin played a big part in my life according to the aura essences numerology. Well, in my own life I had to understand why I went through what I did and having compassion for all involved was important too. Synchronistically, I had received a Quan Yin watch from a client. The lady of compassion.

⁓

I was holding an aura essence creativity equilibrium bottle at my heart centre, with my eyes closed, I could see the soul magenta colour with a foetus on inner of this colour. How amazing! My vision was showing me rebirthing to the next level.

⁓⁓*What Was In Store For Me Next?* ⁓⁓

The following week I had the vision of an eagle carrying prey, a bird, a business shoe followed and a lotus with a star which is the meaning of my name. Seconds later I was also shown a business shoe and a romantic couple. During this time, I had a sense of a beautiful relaxed feeling, a confidence, the knowing that I will be successful in my business knowing that it would be pure. I will bring enlightenment to those who it may resonate with. Only those will arrive. I also felt there would be love and romance in my work. Did this mean that I would meet a spiritual person who recognised my work. It is that love that is pure and beyond the physical. This relationship would be for the higher good of working to the purest level as healers. I was to go and retreat as I could see such a place, where the wisdom would come to me. What prophecy will I receive? At this moment I also saw Onch, my gorilla spirit animal keeping me safe and showing me there was strength within me. How comforting was that.

Onch My Gorilla Spirit Guide

Coming into late October and the weather had changed from mild summer to very autumnal, how amazing it is to see such beautiful colours of the autumn trees, the hedges and leaves falling just like snow flakes. My meditation revealed I needed to keep my fitness levels to an average, some movement without too much exhaustion. The eagle was still soaring this went on for some days now. How exciting.

CHAPTER 8

~~~*The Jurassic Coast*~~~

We had taken our autumn break down to the south of England, this was what was named as the Jurassic Coast. Aha can you remember I mentioned seeing dinosaurs earlier? The angels were telling me this is where I was to come. I self-healed for 10 minutes in the accommodation to give me healing energy to walk to the beach. The shore line seamed a little rough, the waves flowing on to the sand. The Jurassic coast line was astonishing as you could almost see the history behind this primordial landscape. Had this earth really been here for millenniums? We are merely a speck in the whole scheme of things. Speck of minute humanity creating pollution and destruction to the planet that has survived and survived. Walking to the first available rock I felt the wind sweeping my hair at the sides of my face. I made sure I had my hat on and my chest was warm as I was susceptible to the wind going through my body causing me pleuritic chest pains. As I sat on the rock some twenty metres away, I closed my eyes, my meditation had started. I was basking in the autumn sun. It was pleasant meditating in the sun. I also took a stroll to the sea and dipped my feet in, surprisingly the sea was not that cold. I called upon the Mahatma energy and a golden heart appeared in my closed eye view. I also saw Princess Diana at this stage. She seemed beautiful as ever her appearance was from the 1980's. The princess's hair was shoulder length, all flicked back. Her face on the side view as she smiled shyly. The world had much love for her. On one note I felt happy for seeing her and on another I felt the sadness of the world. We had lost one of the most beautiful iconic ladies of our time. What she brought to the world will never be replaced, a soul powerful and yet vulnerable. A deep sigh and a moment to shed a tear. We are all born and we must all die. What happened to Princess Diana taught the world something, she was strong to stand up for her own beliefs eventually, although vulnerable, a person with so much compassion to give to humanity, what does this teach us? This was the most important part of the day for me. During the night I meditated again, which took me into a deep sleep. A vision appeared of a sign. It was a marker sign post pointing to a path. Then a Celtic helmet appeared. I felt as though I was being guided to an ancient sight. Not forgetting I was already at the Jurassic Coast. There are 190 hills in the area and a burial site just around the corner from where we were staying.

The next day we went to the local restaurant for our evening meal. As I was standing at the bar ordering our meal, I recognised a man we saw in Scotland a while back on our trip to Aviemore. He was the man that had 3 or 4 boys with him at a youth hostel we stayed in Scotland. Which I refer to in my first book. On our Scottish trip, on the last day I gave him our four-pint carton of milk as we were departing. This gentleman appreciated it and it was consumed. Now, I was 100% sure it was him but I was a bit weary of what my family would think if I spoke with him, I told the family of this man and eventually I was dared to ask him if it was him. I felt confident so I approached the man. As we spoke, I asked him where we had met before. He was thinking and thinking I gave him clues of where we had already met. He gently touched my arm as the realisation came to him. What a great synchronistic meeting the second time round. The gentleman told me how much he appreciated the milk. My family also then realised it was true as to whom he was. I knew this was a great synchronistic meeting second time round. What are the chances? This gentleman enquired as to what we were doing at this place, I said we had a group of us family members here on holiday at Seatown. This man told us about the coast being full of fossils. He guided us to the place where ammonites could be found. I had already said that the children would be very interested in them. We said our goodbyes and re-joined our families.

The next day Daren, his brother, the children and I took a walk along the beach. I would only walk to the length I could, it all has to be with ease. I was determined to bathe my feet in the sea to cleanse body mind and spirit. Even though it was rather cold I was determined to do this. I sat on the rocks and took my shoes and socks off. Gingerly taking my steps, the pebbled beach was like walking on glass, I tried to put the thought out of mind for it was only a little sacrifice. Can we not make a little sacrifice for our own soul? A little bit of pain to cleanse out that is all. I also thought about the poorer people with no shoes, imagine how life had shaped them, making do without. I even thought I could get used to the pain underneath my feet. However, I was making sure not to slip as I still had my aches and pains, I didn't want to make it worse.

The sun was glaring but the coolness of the wind coming from East to West was prominent. The children were away in a world of their own fossil hunting, as I was in my own, cleansing.

I was ready now to put my shoes on to walk towards Daren and the children. Tristen had found some beautiful clear quartz crystals embedded in the formation of the cliffside. I instantly asked him if he would get some for me. It was our own natural find. I was excited but knew I needed to ask the earth if it was all right for me to take a piece and thank the earth too. It was amazing as Tristen just put his hand into the earth and a piece gently fell away. I couldn't believe it, it was in the shape of wings.

I stood amazed further away from the cliff and could see how astonishingly old this coast was, you could see the fossils that had laid there for millions of years.

I then sensed someone watching me. It took me a good few seconds before I realised who it was. He wore a hat, dark sunglasses with all the walking gear on carrying a hand carved walking stick and a rucksack on the back. Yes, it was the man from the restaurant the other night. His name was Ian as we acquainted ourselves yet again. Hhhmm, third accidental meeting. Ian told me his son Saul was digging away a little further away for fossils. We chatted to say it was another strange meeting. We talked about the fossils and how amazing they were. I was now aware I was being drained of energy. I had looked and checked the time; I had been out of the accommodation for nearly two hours. I excused myself as I made my way back to the caravan park. I knew my signs of feeling unwell and I knew I needed to gently get back. I sat on the steps of the caravan sheltered from the wind. I started to meditate in the view looking out to the beautiful ocean with the sun glaring on it. I felt at peace. Eventually closing my eyes, I sat fixed in this area, I could hear people walking past but I was so engrossed in the meditation.

Tristen and Alysha had made friends on this holiday, Grace was her name. Grace's mum was on her way out. I told Sharon I could feel her heartache, although unaware of what it could be.

The next morning, we set off to see the Cerne Abass Giant. On our way there we turned on the radio, we heard about the nine ladies, it's in the peak district. The nine ladies were graffitied by Fathers of Justice Campaign, it must be devastating for those fathers not having the rights to see their children and many other problems that comes with this subject matter. We were amazed seeing the hillside figure of the giant, also had a little giggle. We went on to Weymouth. On the way we continued to listen to the radio catching up on the latest news.

We were nearly at the end of this holiday and I wanted to continue my fitness, just like my visions told me that night before coming on this holiday. I was proud of my exercise I was getting every day. My cleansing and meditations were going well too. This particular morning, I decided to go for a walk on my own. I did get a little lost, but not overly worried. I could still see the beautiful campsite. The exit I wanted to take was a dead end, which meant I needed to climb a small tree and get over a barbed wire fence. At first, I thought this was too adventurous for me. I knew I had to just do it. Or walk all the way back. Well, I made the jump down. I felt proud and continued walking noticing that all the cows and bulls were in the field. Bravely like never before I prayed that I could make my way through the gate, scared of the animals attacking me, before now we have been chased by cows. I have always been scared when doing this year's previously with Daren, now on my own I could feel my heart beating away, but I tried to keep my cool. Walking on through they were everywhere. But I did it. I made my way back. It was an adventure for me. I need to get my courage back as my messages had been telling me.

~~~November~~~

Coming into November I had my next Angel Evening. Now people were learning on Ascended Masters as I felt that the awareness needed to be out there, of who they are and why the knowledge needs to be shared. During the meditation the ladies that attended said they had heart palpitations; a pain, then release sensations. There was a sense of detoxifying for some. I saw a crescent moon; this was symbolising new beginnings for all. My next vision was a huge cathedral of light. I was standing tall with light beings; all I could see were eyes. Then I saw an eagle fly off then I saw a pair of scissors to cut cords.

～

I was learning about how more grounded I needed to be. My card was telling me I here and now confirm all that is positive in my life, moment to moment. I felt there was a learning for me over the past three days. I felt much more grounded and in the right place in life. People were entering my life to teach me lessons so I would become stronger. I am aware that every ego needs to be balanced as I had already seen this in those whom were spiritual service workers. I needed to now detach from the recent goings on and persist with my life purpose.

～

I had taken Alysha to the swimming baths and I bumped into H, she couldn't believe it as she was thinking of me at the same time. She wanted to chat with me, she felt I was not grounded and I felt I was, but took it on board. We arranged to meet in a few days.

～

I had an interesting evening as it was bonfire night and the venue we attended, were short staffed, so I voluntarily decided to support them as we knew the establishment owners. They very much appreciated our help. It was not that difficult to help. I felt quite energised by this actually.

～

Occasionally people cancelled their appointments for healing but I was quite happy to go with the flow. I was talking to the receptionist in the new physiotherapy clinic I started working from. She had something about her, I saw her as a priestess. If you saw her you would say the same, she was tall slender with flowing blonde hair. The more she talked to me the more I felt tired. We were talking about health and I was telling her about my condition of fibromyalgia and chronic fatigue. She opened up and told me she has the same. She struggles with this too. This lady needed an income therefore had to work a couple of days a week. She knew this job was going to be temporary and so did I. I told her the same that things will shift. She said she had bought some angel cards recently and they were telling her she was a healer. My point was this too. I informed her healing would be good for her as it has helped me so much recently too. She then insisted she must come and see me. L had come for healing she had fallen of a horse. I felt her etheric gap was open. This is situated towards the bottom left of the ribcage. The etheric gap holds the past trauma, I felt the past needed healing for her but not on this occasion. The healing was good for L but she needed physiotherapy too. It was funny as I saw a client not so long before this treatment and I saw a lady falling off a horse. That lady did have horses. But she said she had never fallen off a horse. Maybe I was receiving the information for the future for someone, not the lady in question who had the treatment who never had fallen off a horse. I think this was about L, L enjoyed her treatment and off she went with things to think about.

~

Now I was being guided to books. We went to take Alysha to the library for her school work, but I came away with four books. This was now interesting as I was drawn to a book on psychic abilities, I was looking into this book to see how I was getting my information. I also had a book on fengshui.

The fengshui was all about where I was placing things in my home. One thing my sister did not like about my house was that I had a mirror facing the living room door. She constantly said it was a bad omen. I was unsure of the mirror at times as it had 2 entwined serpents, it was a mysterious mirror. It cost a lot of money therefore I did not want to get rid of it.

~

I had a dream about my aura essence teacher in a red shirt and blue jeans, I also saw his lady friend M, she appeared a little older in the vision. I also saw a lady called Est sitting on the bed, the more I looked at her the more she looked too calm, was it really her? I wasn't sure now as visually it was her but she seemed transformed to calmness, prior seeing her in reality she wasn't that calm. Maybe there were some changes to come with this vision.

~

The healing for Lyn was taking place she was given a name for her guardian angel as I took her through the process of connecting. Lyn also felt the effect of becoming her higher self, she felt her heart beat faster and faster, she felt a lot of releasing through this too. Lyn wanted the St Germain essence in her aura which she needed just lately to help her through her transformations. The amazing thing was that I felt St Germain's hands cup mine as they were placed over her solar plexus. She felt the areas where healing was going. She went away feeling lighter and feeling of release.

After Lyn had left, I decided to do a meditation but I struggled. Maybe we had done enough for the day. I did some research into Dr Lipton's book then my solar plexus started spinning very fast, I was feeling fearful for some reason. This will be explained later. I received a call from Est. She had a proposal for me. But I felt I could not take this on as the first part was not fully fulfilled. After this I could not sleep all night, it was not bad but the visions were amazing. I saw mosaics, esoteric shapes, also the swirl partly looking like the Cho Ku Rei Reiki symbol. I was also shown a coded plan of animals and wildlife, quite difficult to explain really but it was similar to the kabbalah tree of life grid, but animals on it. On the recent aura essences course I was getting visions of butterfly and sea essences. I don't know why that was. I am sure I will find out in the future. My cards were telling me that I should be joyful as there is some amazing force working alongside me, it's a fertile time for projects I must write. The message also was that I do not need to be part of people's dramas. The sense of doing some body work will be good for me such as yoga. I would love to do yoga but will have to find the right person whom understands energy and the way I feel at times with lack of energy. My messages were coming in fast about being a teacher and having the qualities to teach and with this there will be prosperous times ahead.

~~~*The Meeting With The Doctors*~~~

This was the day that I would have my meeting with General Practitioners from the medical sector, our doctors. After asking one of the key doctors if I could speak about healing to them in their Staff Training Day they said yes. I was hoping to do a ten-minute meditation and speaking about how healing can be very supportive as it had been for me. I thought I would have been allowed 20-30 minutes but when I got there it all changed. I was only allowed a few minutes. The doctor who took me in to the room was fine and welcomed me but also said they had lots to cover in the session today and if I could make it brief. I was fine with this as I also know doctors can be busy. As soon as I entered the room my voice went shaky, not normally like this. I was not feeling that nervous so why this was happening I do not know. I suppose this was because I was wondering how to get everything said in 5 minutes. I handed out flyers about how certain doctors in various parts of the country accept healing modalities in the NHS. This is what all doctors need to see as we know it works. My own doctor knew my story he nodded all the way through to support me. It was like having his approval, this was great for me he had seen me struggle for two years, the same doctor whom kept sending me back into hospital as he knew there was something more seriously wrong with me. Some were not happy as I could see the look on their faces some were open to try. I even gave the options for the doctors to come and have a session to see how each doctor would feel with it. I even told them that the two new medical centres should have complementary therapies to support patients. The doctor whom was head of the surgery did say they would need to research more into this as it was not that simple. I proposed that therapies should be available free on NHS. The head doctor did say that he would look into funding. I had my five minutes of speaking and now needed to leave the doctors to continue with other matters of importance. I felt that this would not be as successful at the time. Would they really look into all this? I had done what I needed to, maybe even to plant the seed.

~~~*Meeting H*~~~

Well, I met H and she said things that made me feel incompetent. She said she had concerns over me. I asked her a little later in this same meeting why so. She pulled out a list. She was judging me saying that people charge too much for courses and so on. So, I agreed with her I said I had also seen on the internet courses costing £1,000. She then commented on my procedure and training. I was not as you can imagine happy with this, was there a frustration from H, as a new person had come into the area to share some Angelic Light? I felt her heartache, I was picking up pain in the right side of head. However, I did feel she got the wrong impression about me. But I did listen to what she said about me in case I was wrong.

After this meeting with H, I asked why H had come into my life. The answer came like this, that I was in a process of learning from this. This was also a healing of the deepest fears, I felt this was true as I also stood my ground with her, fear of being told that I do not know anything, by someone I hardly knew. Remember not so long back when I said my solar plexus was spinning and I felt fear? This was the fear. More answers were coming that I have a lot to share as I stand with my head in heaven and feet on earth as long as I rest my attention on the centre of my being. Energy is coming in through communication, there are no limits but there could be tests of faith, this is probably what the beings of light were telling me.

Another lady who attended the meditation class H was talking about disagreed with what was said. She said everything was fine and in control.

CHAPTER 9

~~~The Unexpected Meeting~~~

The next day I attended a local event with Lyn my friend. I heard someone call my name, I started to get tightness in my solar plexus, I felt rather uncomfortable, it was that young man who used to heal me. I was not expecting to see him. He hugged me and asked how I was getting along in life. I told him very confidently I was doing very well, happy and stable and focussed on my life mission. I showed him my book flyer as it was hot off the press, as one would say. He looked at it, as I showed it, I was proud of my achievement and that I was in control of what was happening in my life. I can let the feeling go now of being abandoned during my healing journey.

~~~Georgia's Healing~~~

Little Georgia continued coming for her healings with me, remember she lost her father not so long ago. Georgia regularly had a feeling of a hand on her shoulder. I did explain to her it was probably her father and she would be kept safe. She felt good with this. But it was the grief she had too. Her father appeared in the healing I asked if it was him the answer was yes. I knew it was him I asked him if he had a message for Georgia nothing verbal was said but there was a rush of love pouring through to her, I could definitely sense this. It was so beautiful. Georgia did come back and say that she had no longer felt the hand on her shoulder. I felt he wanted her to be reassured. He was around her in her difficult times though. I also felt his soul wanted to be free too. Georgia's healings had been regular and another time when she came for her session, she became very emotional, I felt her three years of hurt, anger, frustration and more grief pile out. My own heart was crying for her. What an immense amount of sorrow for her to carry at such a young age. By all means her mother was very supportive and did everything she could to help her own daughter through such loss. Georgia felt it was unfair for her father to pass away and leave her. She also felt her twin sister's presence around her. This day was a jittery day I felt for the innocent young child. She talked much about losing her real self since reception class. She did not like the child she had become. Now these are deep words for such a young girl. She amazed me often as she spoke like an adult. She explained that her twin sister would come and see her and would stand and wave at her. She said she could feel her stroking her. She knew this was her sister not just any girl standing waving at her from the spiritual world, amazingly she was always right. The words were touching about her sister, when she said, "She will always have a place in my heart." I was amazed at her empathy and knowledge. During each healing session Georgia would describe an energy flowing down her body. She called it vibration. How would a child at that age know the word vibration or even what it is? She was accurate in her description as what she was receiving was Divine Vibration.

~~~Dreams~~~

Now as you are aware the visions were very easily brought to my consciousness and for very good reasons. But my dreams were very real like too. I had a lot of reoccurring dreams. One dream I had was of one of the doctors and he was not looking well. The doctor who said he would look to see if there was any funding decided he wasn't going ahead with the angel healings. In the dream he said if someone dies from the healings it will be classed as black magic. Anyone who has been a healer in a previous lifetime will feel persecuted for their work and passion. When we are healing with pure energy, we know it's a natural healing system working with the persons soul energy. I had dreams of snakes all over me, during this dream I was being brave but scared at the same time. I received a message "we love wise ones." I also had a dream of the first clinic I worked at and the lady was crying. You will hear more of my dreams further on.

~~~*Helping Others*~~~

My neighbour Sue called round, she saw my beautiful aura essence bottles on Daren's grandad's old sideboard. I decided to ask her if she wanted a quick consultation and she was intrigued. She understood it was God speaking through me as that's how she expressed the reading was. She may have said that as she felt the words were what she needed to hear via her chosen bottles. I am sure Christ was one of her bottles. She asked me what I saw Christ as. I told her what my belief was and that we all understand in our own way, but ultimately same meaning.

~

I was in the bathroom one morning and I could see the door handle turning. I thought it was Alysha opening the door. When I opened the door, no one was there, the children were still in their beds. My son's bedroom was next to the bathroom he also said he heard the door handle turning. Spooky?

~

Now two people had contacted me about their mothers passing away. J and D had come for confirmation that their mother was safe where she was after passing. It was comfort and reassurance people wanted. My own experience with people passing over was intense and the understanding and compassion with that was growing. It was okay as I could handle it. Souls who had passed away found their way to my house; it was always a common thread.

~

M was in a distraught situation. Daren and I decided to help him. I had been sensing a soul around our house for days now, the door handles turning and someone following me around. I told Daren I was certain it was M's mother. We helped M and he was in our care for a very short while. I knew I had to tell him to come and see me on a one-to-one basis, which he did I explained about his mother being around and he took it well. He received the healing he needed and appreciated our help. He managed to keep well after this session. His perceptions had changed and he made a new life for himself.

~

I asked the angels what they had in store for me and I saw an eagle and a gold flash of light. In the night I had visions of Egyptian hieroglyphs, I was hoping to remember them in the morning but I could not recall them, I was a little unhappy about this. I had visions of going out on a romantic night out. I was receiving information for another client to tell her that her grandchild was a rainbow child, she is a little overactive but very clever, this was sure to bring tears to her eyes. Others came for healing too. The 19-year-old girl I was waiting for K finally arrived for her healing she became tearful. She had not experienced anything such as this. K's grandmother appeared in the healing watching over her. This treatment was very much enjoyed and another appointment was booked.

~

Now my niece was struggling with her health and learning about her mother whom died when she was a baby. As you can imagine how hard this would be for anyone who has lost their parent tragically and at a very young age. She was desperate to find answers to what her mother was like, she needed to know and this was the only way forward. She was soul searching too. This was a very difficult situation to help anyone deal with a loss within the family. I loved to talk about my sister, as and when the subject would come up even though for years it was a taboo subject, too much pain to talk of what happened. Yet that would be the greatest healer, to talk.

~

Things were picking up for me now as I was keeping my memory in good tact after all the pain I went through. I learned the first 25 bottles in the aura essences system in 1 hour. I am progressing. I even continued my exercising it was self-rehabilitation. I enjoyed my small walk under the moonlight and stars.

I tried to come back to as many normal activities with family as possible. Something exciting is going to happen. Mid November and I decided to take Alysha to the cinemas to watch Stardust. What a film. Now the name Tristen is quite an unheard name. In this film there was a young man named Tristan I could not believe it. He was the main character. I was very excited already and the film just started. In the film it was said that people want to be someone else when they should be happy with themselves. The power of the star was greatly portrayed in the film. There was a clear message of The Divine showing polarities of light and dark and how light shines so brightly. My thoughts were the same about the light shining with joy. I sat and cried as I felt so overwhelmed by this movie. I thanked The Divine for the clear and beautiful messages that will be passed on to children. The children of our future. In the night I saw a seal on a rock and crow. The seal was telling me to pay attention to the inner voice and having a strong feminine imagination which would help my creative talents, keeping movement going all to do with my balance too. The crow message was telling me I have the ability to move in space and time, this is almost like primordial energy, or an energy that goes beyond time and space should I say. I will need to be aware of unethical behaviour, ok I am sure that will make sense in the future too. I was getting confirmation, of carrying souls from darkness into light and working in the future to assist those who want to release fear. I spoke regularly with Lyn as she understood my journey, she said my challenge will be jealousy. Now this I did not understand, for goodness sake I am only doing what I feel I should be doing. She said there will be lots of this, straight away I said I am not looking forward to that time.

~

My angel evenings soon came round. It was still early days and my family did not always understand what I was doing and why. I felt, they may feel left out or maybe had lack of understanding. I needed space when I was preparing for the evenings, as these times were important to me. As the family did not want to enter this arena fully it made it slight bit difficult for me. Also, my home was used as a public event which I needed to mindful of. But I loved my new passion and mission I should continue the angels work, that's my mission. The angel evening went well. The people whom attended described their guardian angels and they were given names too. We did have a fun time as we laughed at some descriptions. Some of the names the participants had for their angels were Aeron, Michael, Gabriel, Lucinda and Kyle. Some did not get the names. The banter was good which lifted everyone's mood. Some felt they had an idea of the angel being more male like. We enjoyed the united communication of individual angels. There was a lady called Elaine, she said she had an amazing experience of Christ in the room. She reflected that in her occupation, as the elderly were dying their loved ones were coming to receive them. There would be some people who did not believe in the work I was doing with the Angelic Beings and maybe did not accept the spirit world. The young girl whom attended as her mother had asked her to said she only felt relaxed until a certain part of the evening when I guided people through a meditation and she broke down crying. I tried to comfort her. She wanted to tell us about her experience but could not speak the words, she cried and broke down each time she tried to speak. The light had obviously touched the core of her being. During this two-hour evening of pleasant atmosphere, tears of happiness connecting with passed loved ones, guardian angels' connections, everyone received something even if they were sceptical when they first arrived.

CHAPTER 10

~~~*Wings Of Change*~~~

Coming towards the end of November I felt elated. In the middle of the night, I was awoken to be shown a pure white light a bird, and a heart. The words that followed were WINGS OF CHANGE. I was shown on a TV screen a green walk way, a path and a person walking along. Then another vision of beings in white opening their arms and welcoming me.

~~

I had been meditating in the day as I saw Victoria who was the innovator of aura essences. It was so beautiful. There is much beautiful history as why the life changing colour system is in the here and now. But I have wondered who is really ready for this system? Not many people knew how it worked or even what it was. It had brought me much support through my chronic fatigue. I often used the red pomander to boost my energy and strength, most of the time every 20 minutes. It helped me to get some energy and strength to be able to get to the bathroom and to even get off the sofa or bed. Maybe others will understand how these colour energies work all in good time. I never under estimate this system. My children and their friends loved looking at the bottle collection I had in my house it was the main feature in my kitchen. Delight is not the word. Vibrant colours of liquid light.

Tristen had a few friends over one day. They were interested in the equilibrium bottles. Each boy chose a bottle. I did short quick readings for them. They said how accurate it was. They were impressed and said

Parveen Smith

the bottle resembled them. At this time, I was on cloud nine as those youngsters became so interested.

~

Now I was asked by another business to go and join them in their staff meeting. They wanted me to join their practice as one of the directors could see potential. After this conversation my throat chakra closed up, it was becoming difficult to swallow. I was wondering why this was? I had the message earlier about walking away and light beings opening their arms. But why my throat?

I was now looking at recovering, but only in good time. I meditated just about everywhere I went.

I was shown an eagle, owl flying with human face, I know it might sound strange as you visualise what I am saying but that's how the messages appeared for me and I could make sense of this. The eagle telling me to soar, to be free, to have courage and strength too. Was I feeling stifled is a question, was I not using my full potential at the clinic I was at? I know my contract held me down a bit. I am usually a free spirit and like to be open to possibilities is this what I was being guided towards? The owl was telling me to be wise and move through times. Also, that I could see beyond. Also, in this night time vision, I was shown a star which is part of my name, a question mark and a W. I did not grasp the meaning of W. I then saw inside of an office, a room, I could see a computer set up, dark wood and a black fire place which was quite a bit like my osteopaths' clinic.

~~~Receiving Angel Messages~~~

The Archangels were bringing messages. Archangel Metatron had some amazing connections now with my energy being transformed to the next levels in spirituality, I could hear this intuitive message. I only had a thought of him in my mind and then I got these words coming to me "Clear and open your chakras using sacred geometric shapes". I understood this as being attuned to angel healings this happens in the attunements anyway. I was also told to listen to my true feelings, now is the time to summon up my spiritual strength and power and put my authority into action. Ask for guidance and signs, then see my manifestations to the highest possible level. This seemed somewhat beyond me, but I listened. I now asked for the power which God had given me. Archangel Gabriel gave me the message almost like an affirmation, "I embrace my power in a loving way and use it for greater good. Any self-doubt that I may have will be replaced with increased desire to serve, help and teach. Focus on my strengths and many lessons I have learned. I am a living example of following one's Divine guidance."

I was receiving more messages about people's lives in dreams, even of my future boss, knowing of a relationship that was not going to work out for him. During my healing sessions I saw clear images of all zoo animals being set free. I was partaking in this scene freeing them, quite amazing how would I do that I wondered in reality. Or they probably will be looked after in the future.

May the soul you have, be in forever peace, something that all humans are searching for. Life is wonderful a privilege to be alive, to be able to breathe the air and feel loved in a way that many human beings have not experienced. Life is a wonderous journey.

Many people in younger years may go for looks in a person and admire the beauty. Now I see beyond looks and see the beauty within. The soul that holds that beauty. Now I see the colourful souls individually thank you to my aura essences teacher Will I Am, whom gave me the opportunity to come on this colour journey.

~

More and more synchronicities happened but never are taken for granted. People were contacting people that knew me, yet they were only those I had met in recent times through my transformation. I told Steve in my local book shop that I had written a book. He said it would be great to do a book signing as he was working with this idea. He had already had a series of signings taken place. This was exciting new experience for me.

~

Sometimes families drift apart and it sure does happen for various reasons. My sister had not visited for a while and it was coming to the festive season, she sent her husband and children only which I felt saddened about. I felt it was because of me she did not attend. Maybe I spoke too much about my journey and how angels speak with me and show me things. This was originally her interest prior to my illness. But I never asked for the relationship to be this way, maybe some misunderstandings. I felt it was sad it came to this.

~

I had to now pick up my aura essences stock from Will, from my own consultation that I had. I should have been using the equilibrium bottle Guardian Angel Comes To Earth. But I was drawn to Archangel Michael. As I felt I needed his protection and discernment. Will took me to his dungeon as he called it but not a dungeon at all only a delight of all his stock of essences. We looked at the possible bottles I should take away. As I enquired about Archangel Michael tester bottle, it fell out of the pack. I was definitely getting the message. I needed Archangel Michael. So, this is what was bought.

~

Now I was at the stage where I needed to tell the owner of the clinic I was currently working at, that I am going through a transitional phase and I need to continue to move forward on my journey. I was given an ultimatum and I chose to take the ultimatum to leave the clinic so that I could progress further in my spiritual journey to help people. This person was not impressed with my decision. She said that I could be coming from ego to expand just to gain more clients. That is a future plan for anyone whom self invests in a project, am I wrong? For now, I was doing what I needed to with my guidance of walking along a path into the light. Expansion in more than one way. I was given the date 21st 12 2012 and that is what I needed to be working towards not everything is clear at times but this was the message for me in my visions. It was not about becoming egotistical for wealth. She did not understand me and I felt she was holding me back from progressing. After a few words we went our separate ways. There doesn't need to be disharmony and I didn't want that at all. Funnily a girl called Emma whom looked like a fairy as always, said she had seen my wing being bent back and she straightened it for me.

This in a metaphorical situation, that was what was happening for me in reality. This was my message days earlier to have courage and strength as I could see beyond. I asked the angels to help me stick up for my beliefs. I was upset over this and no doubt the other person involved was too. I was not in any real sense here to harm anyone. But I felt a great heaviness in my heart chakra during this time. I spoke to Lyn about this, my great listener. She said the angels knew exactly where to take me. This is when I actually felt the power in the words and I cried. I also asked my angels if I had done the right thing, I got a tick sign for yes. I did a card reading for myself and the cards revealed I have to re-evaluate my life and my beliefs, look towards a new sense of hope in the midst of what has happened, focus upon my strengths, balance home life and choose peace, I am able to see the situation correctly and let go of self-doubt or others doubts. I was seeing this correctly and I HAD DONE THE RIGHT THING. That was not me typing just then, it was as like something took over my hands but written so boldly. Hhhmm.

Later on, when I was resting, I started to get alarming pain in my chest which I knew wasn't my pain I started to do self-healing to get rid of the energy and I could see a man who was a friend in a circle of people I knew of. I also saw Paula's dads face during this time his wife sadly passed away not so long ago. Usually when I saw people in this way its because something was not right with them. As the healing continued it all became better. I felt as an empath this was part of my journey. As long as I could heal it away that's all I could do. On occasions if I knew the person, I would pass on a reminder for them to look after themselves. I saw many more visions in the night the reoccurring ones of the ocean and big fish swallowing little fish. I saw Jesus Christ from behind he said "Follow Me."

~~~Life Takes An Upward Turn~~~

Amazingly I was also invited to do talks and book signings. I did lots of book signings around the country, in various bookstores. I met lots of lovely people. I went back to the same venues throughout the year for more signings. Many staff members whom were not aware of spirituality were coming up asking about the book and what happened to me, also if I had any messages for them which I did. They were happy with the messages.

I received a phone call from a magazine, I called them back they wanted to do an interview piece on my journey. I was quite honoured. This was a time when I was not fully recovered. I remember the magazine wanted my story there and then they needed a photograph instantly so my daughter's boyfriend took it. It was a family photo, as they requested it. This image was then to become an overall recognisable image of me for the future apparently. I was then receiving phone calls from radio stations too. They, the spiritual world did say I was going to fly, meaning I would do well and soar like a bird. People would also explain how they had felt energies and some would bring photos to show of orb happenings and one lady took a photo of a real fairy it was actually amazing to see this being in the photo. Many told me how they felt the book was like a healing tool. Some people felt that when they held the book and they felt good. Some people cried reading the book whether it was a relief for them or a spiritual connection of acceptance or an emotional healing. Some said they read it numerous times, some said they would randomly open the page and get a message from that piece of story. I suppose the angel stories and divine energies were in the book.

~~~A Miracle For Me~~~

I woke up one morning. I could not believe my eyes. I had no pain in my body. I touched my skin and my joints, there was no pain. I felt different. I had no fatigue. There was no tiredness. I felt amazingly uplifted. I knew it had all gone. Trust it had all gone. My breathing was much better.

It had passed two years since my illness began. It may have taken the hospital some time to find a slight tracing of the blood clot on my lung, but I knew there was a blockage as I told my doctor. Time and time again my doctor admitted me to hospital, but they kept sending me home, at one point I was told to breathe into a paper bag as they assumed, I was hyperventilating. I knew it wasn't that. When your body is going through something serious, you know it is, you know your body. The antibiotics did not help the lung infection as it was something more than first thought. I needed answers too, what was happening with my body nearly two years previously? Numerous viral infections and pneumonia was what I was told much later. But I felt too ill, even to eat, a mouthful of food was difficult as

I needed to breathe first, I remember sitting at the kitchen table one-time thinking do I breathe or eat. I had tears rolling down my cheeks, I could not do both it was too painful. I felt I was having attacks every minute or so. This was my living nightmare. How am I going to survive this when the doctors are not giving me the answers I needed? Trying to sleep at night was the scariest. I never knew if I would wake up in the morning. So helpless, and scared. That was one of the nights I cried out for help. "God, just somebody help me I don't want to die just yet, My mission is not completed yet."

That was a painful past in more than one way, but just the past. I was now feeling awed by how well I felt. There was a new journey waiting to happen. I could feel it in my bones, as they say.

CHAPTER 11

~~~*Meeting New People*~~~

I started participating in mind body spirit events as I was now trained in aura colour therapy. I was honoured to do consultations and spread the word about this wonderful system which helped me immensely.

I went to an event in Lincolnshire to be a participant in Butterfly and Sea Essences course. The venue was s spiritual retreat, this would be the innovators home of aura essences. A venue where one would stay and participate in courses. The food was always cooked to perfection and with home grown produce. The food was also considered light as well as the house of light.

Amazing things were happening on this course. I met people from different corners of the world. I met Adriana from Italy whom told me about my connection with Quan Yin. I was staying in Quan Yins room! I was dreaming of Quan Yin it was very real. Adriana could see one evening I became very emotional as she told me the story of this female master. It was in resonance of my life story. It was very painful to hear the story as if my own life was being presented to me, so it felt. She gently helped me through this. After a few moments more I felt fine.

I also met Lenka Markova and her Czech Republic party whom came to learn about the essences. They were very lovely people. I sat both levels of the course which greatly and amazingly brought exactly what the essences said they would do. Erik Pelham the innovator and facilitator of the course put us in some scenarios. He put us in large groups and made essences to reflect how each group could feel emotionally once essences was sprayed into the space. It was intense process for all. Erik told everyone about my journey and told them to take time to spend an evening with me. We all did this one evening. Some people were too tired and went to bed early, some stayed to hear some angel stories and my journey. Lenka and her team were very interested. The people from Czech Republic asked if I could spend some time to just sit and meditate with them, which I gladly did. Lenka invited me to Prague to teach angel healings she said it would really help the people. We came up with a plan. Just Divine timing I had just qualified as a teacher now prepared to teach. Now can you see why I was getting the visions of butterfly and sea essences, and the sea animals? Just to bring me here.

~

I was now giving healings to those whom wanted it, my passion grew stronger and stronger. I moved to a new therapy centre as I was offered a place to work. This was a physiotherapy centre in Cheshire. I was very grateful for this opportunity. I was asked to bring in a team of complementary therapists and manage them. It was a delightful job to have. I had time to rest in my conservatory which was my initial healing room, and still had it set up for family healings. Many a time I would lay on the therapy couch either meditating or self-healing. The sun shining through the glass warming the entire body, also a warming sensation to the soul through healings. I healed every day to become well. It worked. Because I was doing well in my health it did not mean stop healing. I still wanted to heal every day, as a teacher of this system I practised what I preached to my students. Healing with angels was my driving force for everything in my life. I had plenty of rest time and pleasure of giving the healing treatments to those whom required them.

~

I did a talk for the fibromyalgia group as they invited me. I explained what this system was. I explained how people have found the benefits of receiving healings from me and how well I had felt. I explained sometimes we look for a cure, but what healing does is heals the mind, body and spirit. I wasn't sure everyone understood it in the room but I had 2 people who understood what I was talking about. It does not necessarily mean to cure but to make whole. Even those suffering with terminal illness can benefit from this system as it brings inner peace ready for transition. Yes, sometimes miracles can happen, some look at life differently after having healing.

~

Many people suffer and my outlook is we don't have to. It is all about how much do we value ourselves. What is important? We can spend money on shoes, bags lots of lovely clothes, have meals out and spend on exterior materialistic objects but what about our soul. Does our soul not need nourishment and nurturing? As you all know by now having the difficulties with my illness, I knew I could not carry on like this, I knew I could not carry on with this debilitating condition. I felt my purpose was much greater in life. I lost my job, my business, I hit an all-time low in every aspect of my life. I almost felt life was not worth living until something extraordinary happened. It was the love of The Angels and Masters. I cried out for help which in time came, but still took me two years to fully recover. I usually say if I can do it so can you.

~~~More Messages Coming Through~~~

"Your job is to do God's Will. Yes, I had to tell you to make you realise, so that you do not deny yourself."

"Focus on your physical well-being"

"Illness teaches us something, it teaches us to slow down"

"In celebrating the power, love and pure awesomeness of The Angelic Kingdom, in that moment of witnessing this my dear ones, you are also celebrating your own power, love and awesomeness. We celebrate you."
~The Archangel Michael~

2011 Message
"Last year was the balance of female and male Christ energy. Cutting ties of the need to heal through suffering, to be crucified. Shifting from

Piscean to Aquarian energy is part of Ascension process. "2011 is your focus on service to the self, every word is a gem speak it."

This message was poignant as Celestial Radio opened in this year 2011. Which I will share the story with you later.

"The world is your oyster." This message was given to me in 2006, now other people were telling me the same.

~

The spiritual teachings were coming along amazingly. I felt so touched to be teaching the very thing that saved my life, angel healings, as well as the essences to give me protection for my aura. I often felt the Ascended Masters around me and I was able to see them when I closed my eyes during the attunements.

~~~Teaching Angel Healings~~~

I taught many people angel healings as I was a master teacher of the system. I had met Kevin the original founder of the system and spoke to him a few times about my journey and how I had to write my first book sharing my experiencing of the system and how I started to feel well. He gave me his blessings as he said that I could talk so positively about my experiences. I did many Mind Body Spirit events around the North and Midlands of the UK and thoroughly enjoyed them and met some amazing people who had become friends, who had also been teaching spirituality for years be it through sound or movement. I loved the events so much firstly doing many on my own then my family also helped out which was lovely. As I went on to teach many people who came my way, I taught from home and other venues.

I remember more vividly one venue I was teaching a practitioner level course and I was seeing the group through their professional practice and I noticed how the colours of people's skin had changed to chakra colours on various parts of their bodies. I then had one of the girls also say something looked different with me. It was a bizarre standstill moment in time, as if everything had paused.

Then we went for our lunch break and I just stood by the hotel television and then I just paused, again something kept me standing still in time. It felt like everything had stopped, or maybe I was not in this same space and time. When the group returned and we sat to discuss the course further in front of me stood a mighty figure he was easily 7 foot tall with long thin hair. The eyes and the eyebrows very sharp and distinct. He was wearing white and I knew instantly this was not someone from the human race but from elsewhere I kept getting Assyrian Master. He was communicating but it was telepathic but I could not explain what he said. I had no idea in fact, but knew some telepathically took place. For a period of time, I heard droning noises in my home it felt like a link to them. I know you might think this is absolutely crazy but I felt there was a connection. We have to also think, we possibly cannot be the only human beings, or living beings in the universe and universes. When I talked about these beings in classes the music would be interrupted, making awareness to the class students I was talking about these beings.

∽

I had the experience now to go further and I had approached a private hospital. The manager there was very interested in me doing my therapies for the hospital patients as I had studied various complementary therapies. I learned a few weeks after he had left, approaching another staff member was not in my favour they had changed their plans. I was excited to bring my therapies into the NHS and Private Sector especially a hospital.

∽

I continued doing my meditation classes and they were every two weeks to monthly and for years this was a good evening as people enjoyed them whether they were held from the family home or other venues. People just loved the meditations as it was as if they were being healed and they kept most people balanced until the next month.

∽

I had been nominated by a women's networking group for being inspirational and overcoming my health problems and wanting to be successful in my healing work. They put my name forward then Business of Commerce came to my home to interview me. I was rather nervous as I didn't know what to expect. They then came back to me to tell me I was nominated and that I will be invited to the Annual Business Awards. I received the letter and I was in the best new business person awards section. I was so nervous about this when it came to it. I had my ball gown dress on as that was the dress code. We had a 3 course sit down meal. We were sat on a very large round table with other different businesses. The nerves had slowly festered in, I started asking for the angels to help me. Everyone on our table was lovely as we exchanged business cards. On the main screen at the front of the hall they had the nominated groups written on.

When it came to small new business person of the year nominations my name was called over the microphone with Angelic Healing, at that time I thought no one in this room knows probably what angelic healing even means, I had a slight nervous look about me standing out differently to other new businesses such as hairdressers. My husband's palms were sweating due to feeling nervous for me, I think he was more nervous than me, we held hands out of nervousness. They shouted the winner out it wasn't us, but that was ok as we had an incline that the hairdressing businesses stood a greater chance plus at this time healing work was not really heard of in our area.

So as the story goes with my visions, the angels' showed me this was the entrepreneur evening and me in my business shoes having a dinner.

~~~Trudy's Healing~~~

I had lost contact with a friend due to just simply drifting away. Trudy and I met 6 years previously and her husband tragically passed away. We just happened to bump into each other and strangely I asked her to come and see me for a healing session. She had become emotional through the healing session and I knew why. Her deceased husband brought her to me. He wanted to rest in peace and wanted her to let go of him so she could be free too. She listened attentively and began to understand why she was asked to come for the healing session. She appreciated everything that we spoke about, leaving happier and relaxed even though still a bit emotional.

This shows when someone passes over it is a big thing to come to terms with still, even years later.

Trudy came for further healings and her dad probably a sceptic, didn't agree with his wife having a healing. Trudy had read my book and left it on her dad's table. Her dad muttered beneath his breath he had plenty of other books to read. That night he woke up but didn't know why and went downstairs. He was drawn to my book. Then he had a hypo attack as he was a diabetic. He believed that he was drawn to the book so he could wake up, his medication was on the table next to the book. Otherwise in the night he could have died so he told me later. From then on, he went on to read the book and was quite impressed and surprised. He also felt connected to some of the happenings in the book. This gentleman said he enjoyed reading the book and couldn't put it down.

He also became interested in some workshops Lyn, Caroline and I delivered. What a turnaround!

CHAPTER 12

~~~Visions Of 2008~~~

In the January, I appreciated to be able to breathe more easier than the last few years. It was so amazing to just be able to breathe properly again. I was woken up in the night to be shown 'Go With The Flow', and my business shoe, which was all about me taking my business further. I could see the hand of God, its big and with a pure white light around it. One day, Moyra who is a spiritual author had arranged for us to go to London to meet Benjamin Crème and listen to his lectures and take part in transmission meditation. She knew why I had questioned some things I was seeing, I wanted to go purely to meet Benjamin as I wanted to ask him about the TV appearance of Maitreya and about the huge 3d handprint on my mirrored wardrobes. Benjamin Crème had confirmed it was Maitreya. As I listened to the lecture, I saw a huge being of light behind Benjamin and I knew that was Maitreya, the world teacher. At the event I bought some handprint images, one on a very large card.

When I got home from this lecture, I noticed on the back of the image was a write up similar to what I was telling Benjamin it was there in black and white. Maitreya's reappearance in the media. I instantly broke down in tears with the most overwhelming feeling physically, and within my soul. As I wept, I closed my eyes and I could see this image of a rose within the palms of the hands.

In my night meditation I saw a white coffin, of course implying death, with the arrow pointing down but I had no idea what this was leading to.

Karen my niece spoke to me about my book Seeing Is Believing, Believing Is Seeing as she knew someone in the same situation as the Unafraid Story. The person she knew brought the child to me for a few sessions of healing and it really helped the child. The mother was thankful too. Many people who were now opening up to having the healings were feeling peaceful afterwards. The reasons for having the healings definitely were a plus so that one can carry on with their life as peaceful as possible.

～

On 1ˢᵗ March I had a dream that Lyn who is my friend, her husband had a sudden heart attack whilst she was away with me. In this dream his father was with him at that time. James their son was a paramedic. She initially handled the news of his death well. Then grief set in and we both sobbed. What a horrific dream.

～

My next visit with Lyn was today, as I was driving to see her, I became emotional listening to some lyrics 'giving up battle and war' I felt Jesus's energy and the music cut off and came back on. I always had a lot to share with Lyn.

～

Two ladies came to see me, one of them needed to let go of their loved one, who had passed over. They listened attentively. As I spoke to them about the importance of this, then suddenly one of the aura essence bottles exploded. It was the innovator's signature bottle that burst she was the innovator of aura essences I felt that was a potent message itself. We should let people go to the light and release them so we are not holding the souls to the earthly planes, However, the lady who needed to do the letting go phoned back later to do this process to set the soul free. I think she got the understanding of what was for the best.

～

Alysha was scared to bath or shower as she always saw spirits in the bathroom. She described them in detail for example the balloon man he was in the bathroom a lot when she used to go in as soon as she started to run water these spirits would be around. She always said they were real like you and me. Daren got irate at times saying it was my fault the spirits were in the house. He always laughed off things that he couldn't see, calling them ghosts and joked constantly lately. That night I placed angels all around the house and in Alysha's room. I then sent fifteen souls to the light.

~~

A few days later we went to the O2 in London to see Tutankhamen's Tomb Exhibition. I had been interested in the Egyptians and tried to read the complex history. However, I don't think much of the knowledge sunk in. Travelling down I was so very tired for no apparent reason and nearly decided not to go. I had done maximum healing on myself to help me get through the day. I felt like I was going to pass out at the time of going into the room of the tomb. Maybe I was just picking up some really negative vibes of what had happened to Tutankhamen, even though this tomb was probably a replica. Some things I saw in this exhibition also linked with the visions I had during meditations on the master class and with a client who had a healing a few days before. She was also interested in this history, I could see the stone columns, there were at least two rows of column's that I could see at the period of Akhenaten around 1353 BCE.

~~~*Having The Strength*~~~

On this particular day I had been meditating and I could see Erik's face in disappointment and it seemed so real. I had known Erik for a period of time and he helped me also when I went for a reading once, it was for the butterfly and sea essences. I knew I had to see him in person and I travelled three hours to get there. On the way there I nearly had two accidents almost like something was trying to stop me from getting to him. I can remember driving asking for angelic help to keep me safe. I met Erik and his family and they kindly welcomed me in and we had dinner. That evening my body went into shock. Erik kindly looked after me during the evening. This wasn't the first time this had happened. Every time I went to new areas geographically my body went into shock. My reading was very good and he explained why my Divine beings, another aspect of me were working with me to get things done in the world. He explained my mission and where my support was coming from. I could clearly see the vision of both aspects of the female and male divine beings. I left Erik's feeling more content and maybe that's why the negative forces didn't want me to go, so I wouldn't find out who my divine beings were and how they would lead my path to support humanity. Hmmm…..

MY BELOVEDS I STAND HERE BEFORE YOU NOT TO SEE YOU SUFFER BUT TO SURRENDER

Channelled Message from Jesus 12/10/08

The angel evenings I had been holding regularly were amazing as everyone said. Each evening had a theme and this evening was a popular one, it was again about finding out our guardian angels names. Most people got a name. El Morya an ascended master was working with me powerfully this evening and there were lots of confirmations for people in the group. There was a lady called Sarah who had a link with owls, owls are her link to get messages from a deceased loved one. I felt I had to tell Sarah that it might be a good idea to go through the letting go process I did for those who lost loved ones. Sarah had found a dead owl outside her gate this was a little disturbing for her. I felt that the deceased lady friend needed to go to the light. The owl did not have a scratch on it so Sarah said. Her husband decided to bury the owl in the back garden. I was getting messages from this deceased loved one, she was in agony and needed to be released and she was distressed. Since the angel evening, I had been getting left breast pain, I was getting worried why I was getting it so severely and the message from the deceased lady was correct she wanted to go to the light. Sarah agreed that this was distressing, and decided to do this the next day. Finally, the day had come to let go of this lady, Sarah brought her husband with her as they all knew each other and they were all friends. When I was doing the letting go with them, I felt this lady's severe breast pain again and they told me she died from breast cancer. They felt her energy in the room as I did, it was a huge sense of relief. I never got the pain again. I felt I was experiencing this in my body to really get this situation sorted it really could not have gone on any longer, the final letting go was done. Thank God! Within the next night or early morning should I say, in my vision I saw the deceased lady and she was happy; her hair was flowing as she sat on a white horse, visually I could see angel wings around the horse, Pegasus I suppose you can say. Then came a knight and sat on the horse behind her and off they rode together. She was so happy it was almost like she was fulfilled with joy and with another soul. A beautiful ending to this story.

~

My next new client had arrived and she had a tumour visible on the face. It was just so uncanny how this lovely lady was a beauty therapist yet she had a tumour that was quite large and that seemed the opposite of beauty.

She enjoyed her healings. This lady had bought my book from a local book shop and she needed to sort out a situation with someone she worked with and she started writing a letter and randomly stuck it in my book. When she opened the book to get her letter, she saw some key words on the page. She knew she had to finish writing her letter with those words in it to end her distress. She was so passionate about having her sessions she came weekly. During her one-hour session we could visibly see her transformation. Her tumour on her face was getting less. She used to go to the bathroom mirror to check it out and she said it was amazing. Of course, we cannot claim to cure big diseases such as cancer but we saw it shrinking for sure. When she would come again it had gone back to its normal size. So, this lady decided to join the course so she could self-heal daily. She thoroughly enjoyed the course and even revamped her house looking angelic. After a little while I had not heard from this lady. She spoke on the phone sometimes. I decided to call her one day and her husband picked the phone up as I joyfully asked for her. He said "Oh you don't know do you?" I said "know what?" He said "she passed away and right now is her funeral." I immediately lost strength as my legs went like jelly and I crouched down on to the floor with disbelief. I was in total shock. He told me the funeral was happening just now as they were about to leave the house. I was so sad to hear this. I rang the husband a few days later he said the tumour did not cause the death it was a brain problem. I expressed my deepest sympathy and he did say she thought highly of me, all I could do was say how lovely she was and she just wanted to be healthy, he agreed and we said our farewell. A sad story indeed. All I could hope was that she was in a special place.

~

My next publishing company had contacted me, the young girl who spoke to me on the phone was embarking on her spiritual journey. She had given me a few options on taking my next book forward. I was always really enthusiastic and could see my synchronicities. Emma her name was from the publishing company she gave me a nudge to finalise my agreement with them so I consulted my oracle cards and the guidance was, artistic expression, you are seeing this situation accurately, flow of prosperity, drink more water, law of attraction, stay optimistic and helpful person, alchemy, watch my thoughts and blessed change. What more could I have asked for; my guidance was very clear in what I needed to do. I signed up with Author House my new publishing company and paid for my book. Another accomplishment.

~

My cards were telling me of partnership, receive abundance, successful changes and transformations. I was told to let go of fear and go through a rebirth process of mystery and truth and keep the trust in this process. More Poignant messages to be taken on board.

~~~Celestial Radio Was To Be Born In 2011~~~

I had been working at another local radio station as a volunteer offering many valuable hours, as I recovered. I helped run the station as a fundraiser and to get sponsorships. There was a reason why I was offering my time for that last two years almost. I had my own Health and Well Being Show and a Food For Thought Show on this radio station, there was a lot to learn, but as it was community based I felt I could offer my time. Where there is Divine Will there is a way. But everything is a learning curve. Aha you see the word learning? That is exactly what was happening here. Just like many times in my life. I was being used as an instrument. I had already vowed to God that I would be of service, all will become clear a little later.

So as this particular part of the story continues, I knew I had faithful listeners. Other bigger radio stations also listened in to see what my speaking skills were like as individuals told me, they were impressed in the way I held my interviews. Now this was an honour in its own right, beautiful compliments. On the day of leaving, I had phone calls about my shows how people were going to miss me. In total on this very first day, I had three messages from the public. This was confirming I cannot just finish here. In fact, how true this was, as my own soul felt my task was not finished. Maybe not even started. So, this evening I was still somewhat agitated as I told my family of what had happened. I spoke to my closest friend Lyn Harvey. I told her what had happened. I went to bed to have some sleep and I remember falling asleep but what happened next was amazing. I heard a voice say "Celestial Sounds" The voice woke me up in the middle of the night. The voice was neither male or female all I know it was a real voice and I was awake. It was a very clear and kind voice. I was awake thinking what should I do with this. I pondered on it the next morning and telephoned Lyn once again, she said what does it mean for you. I did say to her I was being told to set up my own radio station. It sounded amazing, but a big project, where do I even start, came to my mind. She carried on talking and said you know you have to do it then. My eyes just grew big at that moment. Wow was the only word coming to mind. Lyn said I know you will do it, I agreed with her. Then I went on with my normal work that day and told Daren about the voice and the message he just muttered "uuhh really, ok" well that was quite normal! I think that he thought it would be another angelic message I would just take on board. I did take it on board then I rang a technical engineer whom set up radio stations and I asked if my thought would be possible, he said yes. I started organising things, ordering items I needed. I had everything in order, in a crazy way. Things were just happening so fast; orders being placed left right and centre. I thought the station would be ideal in a summer house. So, I ordered one. My family thought I was going mad yet again, believe me I was not, I was just going full steam ahead with the inspiration and guidance which was coming to me regularly. Dean was the technical guy who was helping me. I put all my financial income into this. Daren and his brother helped to build the summer house, electricians came and did their work. Neighbours probably were curious but my focus was on getting things organised. We worked day and night to put things together.

I was still trying to put the station name together I know the voice said "Celestial Sounds" but that was not all. The title needed the word radio in it. Some people tried to give ideas but none of it resonated. There we go it was to be called Celestial Radio.

I focussed on my task ahead which was Celestial Radio! Within one week I got the sponsors, eight came on board instantly. I now had to work harder than ever. I worked twelve hours a day easily, I put all my own chosen music in for the station giving it the identity as a Health And Well-being Spiritual Radio Station. I worked twenty hours and then one day there was so much to do and only me doing it that I worked twenty-four hours plus. This was the only way the work was going to get done. My family did not quite understand why I was doing this but they knew I was an impulsive person; I went with the flow there and then. The station ran well, the house had got a little neglected from my side as I only had energy to do so much. I was prepared to do this so focus needed to remain on the station, only one person running the whole station and that was me.

I joined some social networking sites and connected with many people from different parts of the world. It was needed for the station to have the full impact. My job was to communicate with many and spread the word about Celestial Radio. The Celestial Sounds were played every day between 10am until midnight. The station was to open between 10am and 10pm initially but as there were demands I opened it until midnight. I got to the point where I needed people to help me, this message came through via one of my Angel Evenings I held in autumn 2011. There I was guided to ask Susie and Lorna. The weeks ahead came along and more and more people joined to present shows on the radio as and when it suited them. Often at the Angel Evenings I asked did anyone else want to join, or I approached people that I thought were able to be part of this new project. I was aware that not all staff will stay forever. It was all to do with their commitments in their own lives too. We stayed as a not-for-profit radio station. I had been seeing the number three for a very long time, now I was seeing double figures on the digital clock 20:20, 21:21 and so on. The messages were getting stronger. My work was getting intense. We were now becoming more and more like an all-ladies radio station probably the first.

We enjoyed calling ourselves an all-ladies radio station, it was about the feminine power if you like. More and more topics and subject matters came in. As we were an interactive station, we had listeners wanting to know more about angels, healing energies, my story too as listeners had known I had written a book. So, I fulfilled listeners requests. I had also interviewed Deva Premal and Mitten, Tim Wheater, Jason Chan, Terry Oldfield, Jsu Garcia, Faye Ripley, Dr Hillary Jones, Alan Jacobs and many more people.

During the first six months of Celestial Radio running, I was able to cherish all the work put in not just by myself but via the new ladies whom joined also. I met some great people from different continents. Some were helped by tuning in at the right time to hear the vital messages for their spiritual growth. Some were brought to tears, some saved their family situations, some were understanding more about their relationships, some were saved from committing suicide. Above all, much information about energy and healing was given. From the meditations alone the listeners were being transformed. One listener from overseas had not really done my meditations before but decided to give it a go. He was looking for a job. After the meditation which was all to do with abundance and projects, he had two jobs presented to him. He was quite amazed as at one stage there was nothing, then there were two opportunities. He then looked further into which was more suitable. I explained to him this was not the first incident like this, other people had also reported back with their thoughts about changes in their lives after listening into Celestial Radio. It was all proving something to me. Months into setting up Celestial Radio I was given the message that Celestial Radio will heal people. It is after all energy, frequency, sound, all connecting worldwide. An amazing opportunity for the angels to do their amazing work. They just needed a human channel to put it into manifestation and reality. Then here we are. Some listeners did not feel it was entirely their cup of tea but that is also acceptable. Some liked more soothing music some liked more upbeat music so this was my job to explain why Celestial Radio was set up. I remember a particular lady who was moving house and was literally living from boxes, as everything was getting packed. The social media interaction allowed me to communicate with her. I asked her to have a listen to Celestial Radio in the background as she is finishing packing, she did just that. Whilst listening she said in the hours she listened in, her whole life story of forty years played for her. She said she cried at some pieces of music then laughed at some. This was honourable for me to hear this, this was her healing journey, what a privilege. I loved that this impact was made for this lady. She was forever thankful. I believe she moved and then carried on with life. Well, you can imagine the healing taking place for this lady.

I was told by someone that Celestial Radio could be the new Opera Winfrey show. I laughed. I thought, oh well cannot complain, take it as a complement.

I remember listeners continually asking me about types of healing and at times I had other experts on to talk about them. For me it was always important to be trained by a reputable teacher. I had many discussions on this on my shows but some may have liked it and some may not have. The truth of the matter is attunements need to be given by a trusted teacher. Not through a book by oneself. We have to maintain integrity for each system as it has been given, there is a danger too many things written on social media sites and the purity is dissolved. That was my belief at this time.

The angels and masters will work with those to the fullest whom maintain purity and integrity.

Another time in the early days of Celestial Radio I remember a listener from India said he was dying from a disease; this was supposed to be an April Fool's joke. Firstly, I was shocked but then believed it. Secondly, when he said he was not I was not happy as I explained to this person please do not say such things as they can come true, your words may be very powerful as you believe in Krishna and pray regularly. Well months later I find out his mother has a problem with her heart and at such a young age she could die. I knew that was instant karma of words. We must choose our words carefully so we don't bring on unwanted Karma.

Doctor Hilary interview was interesting as we talked about prescribed medications and millions of pounds wasted due to medication unused. Also, we talked about negative publicity on medication but Dr Hillary brought another aspect of how many people's lives have been saved by taking medication and indeed I agreed. I asked Doctor Hilary about complementary treatments he agreed they can be helpful but not to replace conventional medicines. I have seen many people's lives saved with conventional medication. As the doctor said you cannot just stop taking medication, advice would be needed on it. Doctor Hilary and I talked about meditation, we also talked about having a reputable reiki practitioner if one was to seek complementary therapies, again and again reiterating my thoughts, a good practitioner. So, it shows that some people will do reiki for not so good reasons and some will for higher purpose. The same goes with any type of healing, choose a pure system.

The Shows went from strength to strength with many listeners enjoying our weekly giveaways, people wanting to be sponsors, live Laura Boyle Reading Shows, food shows, gardening shows, poetry shows, book reviews, the mantra show, live meditation hour, and many more including two children's shows which were a treat, Eleanor and Mitchell were a delight to listen to and it helped their reading skills. We had a local business man who helped us immensely towards getting some radio equipment. We couldn't thank him enough his name was Steve. We had men join us to help get the music in the system every week, they were all very helpful. The local college even asked if we could have work experience for teenagers which I took on two young girls. It also gave confidence to everyone who joined whether they worked behind the scenes or live on shows.

We started getting people contacting us from various charities needing help, I became good friends with some of the charities as they had suffered with disastrous earthquakes, the urge was to really help them and I did just that. I sent money I earned to feed the hungry orphans, to clothe them. It came to the point that I couldn't do this all by myself. I needed to think bigger. So, I started to ask the radio staff to assist. We all helped to put hampers together and auction products, my own town had helped to give donations to raise funds for orphans in The Haiti Earthquake. Hundreds and thousands of people died, so sad it was to hear Les and Reg talk about the disaster on air. I organised different restaurants to help put charity dinner events on so that we could fund raise. They were all very successful. The funds went direct to the charities with no middle man taking funds which was my strong belief system. In the years prior I always donated via big organisations to disaster zones but always felt did my hard-earned money go to where it was needed. One event led to another as the community also enjoyed them. Even to the point where we even had a local person who would do the auctioning for us professionally, it was so much fun but for me a lot of hard work in preparations. The word got out more and more. Zoe a good friend also helped, she rallied round to get books and other things to auction off. She invited many of her friends and nursing colleagues to join in the fun and good causes. The radio brought many people together and even friends for life.

I wondered if the message I got years ago, was this it? The world is your oyster. Many people around the world connecting via Celestial Radio and many people were helped by this spiritual radio station.

~~~*Arnab*~~~

So now to my next story whereby a young man named Arnab from India. He was locked in his bedroom by mistake by his parents. They had gone quite a distance to seek medical support out of town. Meaning it would take them two hours plus. He was a listener to Celestial Radio and I was on air broadcasting. He was now contacting me asking if I could help in anyway. I think he was getting claustrophobic. I sent him some angels and he was communicating with me on social media. He said he was feeling some peace flowing through and didn't have too much fear as it dissipated. He was so very grateful and he calmed right down. His parents returned earlier than expected which relieved him quite a bit.

He then asked me "Are you Parveen Smith? I said "yes I am." He said, "Oh have you written a book called Seeing Is Believing?" I said "That's me." He couldn't believe it as he explained his uncle had bought the book for him as a gift. We both chatted on social media in amazement. Another great synchronicity.

CHAPTER 13

~~~My Own Therapy Centre~~~

During the days of running the radio station I had opened my own therapy centre. It was called Celestial Centre. It was connected to the radio station, Celestial Radio. The lovely volunteers came to support the radio station as a means to keep the station running, we were the only holistic radio station at the time as we knew it. Some of these volunteer staff were also connected to the therapy centre and brought their clients in to heal. It was not the easiest jobs to do to manage therapists and run a station, being in a small town not everyone would be interested in holistic therapies, we all did our best though I am sure. The rent was very high but we balanced it out per therapist. Everyone was in the same boat then equally. During the time the centre ran we ran various events, to make things work.

From the therapy centre I ran some meditation classes and training classes whereby others came in to train the therapists, this was a success too. I was also able to link in with a centre in London and offered my support but it was rather a distance, even though I enjoyed giving my service, the healing helped traumatised children too. We did many world peace meditations and even prior to having the centre we did some powerful world war zone meditations whereby within days those areas had relaxed and the leaders who did injustice to the innocent had their own karma. This left the group quite surprised, what we did worked. In the room during the meditations, I could clearly see what was happening in the war zones and so could others when we shared our thoughts. Intense as it was at the time, we all felt we had spiritually powerfully made a difference. Some may say it was just a coincidence, but I knew the power of what was capable.

During 2012 we also did a powerful meditation. It was on 21/12/12 at 9.12pm. It felt like something very big was coming at this date and I had been getting many numbers consistently prior to this day. I started telling people who I knew and I was working alongside with at the time. It seemed like the world was going to end but it obviously didn't, in fact it was more that we needed to turn the energies into peace. The purpose was to assist in the world not ending but creating a better world. We desired for a world of harmony and peace, no more wars in other countries, innocent people dying constantly, this was upsetting for so many sensitive people watching and knowing what is going on in the world. A lot of spiritual people thought the world was going to end in 2012. Our meditation was powerful and we all felt something had changed that evening. We felt we had spiritually made a difference. We all felt amazing from this night everyone drove home in the depth of the darkness with intense fog, we carefully drove home but barely able to see the cars in front of us just a few feet away. We all said how relieved we all were when we got home safely.

~~~Mother Mary~~~

A group of us went to an ashram in Germany to hear some spiritual lectures and to be blessed as a facilitator of a chanting group. This was a community they had built over time; this was a spiritual organisation. It was a bit like a sanctuary. I can remember it was very cold inside the building but then it was early spring. I was just the observer at this time. I went with the flow. I bumped into one of my Czech students there who ran my angel classes for me in the Czech Republic. I had been into the ashrams catholic church whereby I had the most amazing experience it was as if God had touched me. I felt the presence so overwhelming that I sobbed, nothing could stop me I was completely weakened to the love of God and the purity of the energy of Mother Mary at the same time. I could not stop my tears this went on for over half an hour. I was in awe of what just happened. That was my reason for being in the space just to feel this oneness feeling of purity. I also had no strength in my physical body I can remember that.

~~~*Some Things Do Come True*~~~

Between 22nd to 30th April 2013 I was getting pain in my head and sides, it felt like tingling inside the brain and some pressure. But an amazing sense of expansion, 'vast clear and expansive' were the words given to me as crystal clear. This sounds a very strange way to describe it and it was a strange experience to put all those feelings into that week. The sensations were real but a clarity at the same time as I told my family they laughed at me; they knew I was a bit strange in my descriptions of what was happening to me. Oh well it was the simplest way of describing it.

$\sim\!\!\circ$

On the very next day I had a vison of 210 cyclists then 100 obstacles shown. Everyday I was getting more and more guidance of something yet to come. I was given a time 50 and 54 when I opened my eyes many minutes had passed. What was this time relating to?

$\sim\!\!\circ$

My head pains continued. My second book was coming on well. Celestial Radio staff were so very helpful I had eighteen volunteer staff on and they all did a fabulous job. I was hearing from them how being a part of the station gave them confidence in life, even the two children who presented shows, their confidence grew so their parents said. I had a business man who shared the same building as us who really helped the station, he helped to fund the station and buy us computers. Everyone who could did their best to support the running of the station. I felt so blessed at this time but still lots of work to be done.

I kept feeling something was happening to me I kept releasing excess energy and felt lighter after it. I noticed everywhere I was going and what I was doing was put in front of me, I felt I was driven to my destinations spiritually.

I would bump into people or people would email about my first book saying how they were enjoying it and couldn't put it down. It was continuously the same feedback.

~

I had a lady who I will call Y who loved my colour therapies I did. She used to say I feel I could drink the colour, my body doesn't get enough of it. Every time she had the colour put into her aura and chakras, she used to describe it to depth of how her soul felt and even very emotional too. She started doing readings and wanted to do me a couple, what she came back with stunned me it was about my energy and how I was working celestially. She researched the celestial galaxies and constellation happenings and sent me the images and how she felt the connections were coming back to me. I was quite surprised by this at the time. My name means a cluster of stars which universally shows clusters of large groups of stars in the galaxies. She said she could see me as Paramhansa Yogananda, and my link with him. Even my children said I looked like him.

~

Can you remember the dream about Lyn's husband dying suddenly from heart attack, unfortunately that dream came to reality. Bob, Lyn's husband had a sudden heart attack on 20th July 2014 and died instantly. He went out for a run and Lyn had expected him to be gone half an hour as that's what he told her. He hadn't come back at the time expected so Lyn went out in the car looking for him. She noticed there were three police cars and an ambulance but didn't think too much about it. As she got back, she walked over to the police cars and ambulance, not far from her house, she went over to ask the police what had happened, she told them she was looking for her husband. The police men glanced at one another briefly, she knew it was her husband Bob in the ambulance, he passed away suddenly from a heart attack exactly there. Such a sad, sad time. I was heartbroken for her, what a shock. I helped Lyn as much as I could with her healings. Lyn told me she saw Bob's aura strangely white days before. James their son noticed the same almost like something wasn't right. I gave Lyn bottle

26 from the aura essence to help her with her shock. The funeral was such a sad day seeing my friend go through this awful time.

∼

The vision of the bungalow 4 was a vision and an experience showing me I was to get started with my practice and somethings were good but I also needed to move on, The Divine had other plans for expansion for me.

∼

As my energy had got better physically, I was able to do more and more. I went on a course in Vienna and I met some very lovely people. I thoroughly enjoyed this course; it was a connection of colour and light. On one of the days, I had a very bad experience, my body went into shock, Shano was my teacher and she helped me. It was when we drove through a certain area that I noticed very suddenly I felt very, very ill. I was totally in the moment and I could feel my body shutting down. One of the girls in the taxi said this is a run-down drug area. I felt all the traumas of this area going through my body. When we arrived for dinner that an organic food company were putting on for us to showcase their produce, I just couldn't even sit up. Shano had to hold on to my feet to ground me and used some essences on me. I unfortunately ruined her evening as she needed to stay with me to ground me. I couldn't eat and I couldn't wait to get back to my accommodation. We managed to get through that night just about but I still felt traumatised. When we were working with the beamer light pen, I saw what was happening. I was reliving my childhood and almost like an abandoned feeling from my mother. This was all on a spiritual level. This went on for a couple of days. So much trauma my poor body was feeling at this time. I had not felt this fragile since being unable to breathe with my illness in 2005.

∼

I decided to put a trip together for all angel healing students as a self-appreciation, it was to Barbados. My students were excited about this new venture. Everything was booked and off we went. It was a lovely place to go with the white sands and the sea was amazing even though I have had fear of water all my life. The vast ocean was an overwhelming place for me yet so invigorating and we know how rejuvenating being by the sea can be. My body went into shock once again, all the areas of this lands pains and hurts and fragmentation of the people was going through my body. I could visibly see them all and it was so real like I was taking their shocks away. I could see the people and I felt like I was dying. I can remember continuously telling Lyn and my younger sister that I go through a dying process quite often in places I have never been before. I used to dread going to Leicester and London for these same reasons. The more places I travelled since my recovery the more I had the dying experiences. I feel the fear I had been feeling over time was about this period about how my body will have to cope with fear when experiencing the dying process. It was almost like I was holding on by the last golden thread. This also happened when I felt world disasters happening which I will share more with you in the next book.

～

Whilst writing this last part of the book people are still interested to read my first book. I had a client who was going through cancer she was diagnosed with terminal cancer. I helped this lady through her traumatic time, she had her healings with me. She survived it even though she had terminal cancer she lived a further many years. Sadly though, the cancer came back and she passed away. I felt it was a privilege the angels gave her more years with her family, the last time I saw her she was working again and looked really well. Then as I sit and write the final part of this book, years later, her husband contacts to get a copy of my first book for his new partner as it really helped his deceased wife. The book has been recognised by many as a healing book.

～

The bicycles that I had a vision of in 2013 was the Tour De France that took place in July 2014, a year after my vision. Apparently 198 cyclists in 22 teams of nine would cycle over 21 days to complete 3,500 kilometres. I can remember Sharon my eldest daughter keen to take Jacob, my friends' son to see the Tour De France. The cyclists were to race past our main road. It was such an amazing sight for us. People lined the roads about an hour before reserving their places, some even had brought their chairs to sit on. The local schools also witnessed this historic event.

~∽

Remember the vision of the place in Bulgaria, I spoke to my brother-in-law and he did have to go out to sell the property due to it having too many problems, he could have done without. Looks like they did that just in good timing.

~~~2020~~~

For now, I am going to fast forward to 2020. You will hear more of the divine happenings in the next book.

The year 2020 arrived and I had been giving predictions annually in my meditation classes for years whereby all students I had taught would gather in my house and we would have a wonderful 3-4 hours going through various learnings and sharing how we are progressing. I would bake some cakes for our tea break, which I loved to share healthy cakes.

I held a meditation class in the December 2019 to encourage everyone to find their happiness to create their own happiness. This all made sense for 2020. Whilst the annual prediction was taking place in the January class, I could see Hitler and I was given the message there would be something big coming. We will need to adapt as changes were coming, a bit like a world war, world war 3, but not a world war against people but a different type of war, there will be mass death. I remember when Glenda opened her eyes, saying to me, "Oh Parveen I've just glanced over at that book it says Hitler, can we move it?" Little did she know it all linked to what I was visually seeing. I explained to the group the channelled message, something is going to happen but don't go into fear. There were other messages about politicians and usually how we need to look after our planet.

I was getting visions; it was horrendous to see people dying. Nurses running around frantically. Too many people dying. I even was shown a vision of me being a nurse. Almost like I was to take a role to help in some way. I was shown a clinic like room and people were waiting and I was one of them. People were saying I wonder if she has it or has he got it, this was the virus they were talking about. At one time I was shown this image very clearly, Daren sitting on a cemetery bench crying, but I couldn't see myself. I was wondering if this was my mortality. I was concerned at this stage as I had breathing problems in 2005, I couldn't bear to go through not being able to breathe again.

I had continuous visions for weeks. I only told a few people of my visions at first. I knew there would be a food shortage so in the January I started to put one or two extra items in the trolley, for example, instead of getting one tin of tomatoes it was two tins of tomatoes. I did this weekly. I think my family thought I was going mad as I put the box in the bedroom and kept adding to the box. I told them to do the same but none of them did. One day when we were out shopping in the supermarket, my daughters bumped into Wei Ling my friend. They told her what I was doing she came over to chat and she also put bits of extra things for her children in her trolley. She knew that when I feel something it will happen. My family still didn't quite get the understanding of what was yet to happen. I was aware not to panic everyone I knew. The news bulletins were coming in thick and fast about an outbreak of a virus in China, and it had started to spread to other countries. Doctors and nurses were also dying. The whole world couldn't understand what was going on. Countries after countries being severely affected by this deadly contagious virus. This was like watching an apocalyptic movie. My heart went out to Italy watching the dreadful images on the news seeing people dying with such high mortality figures. The world at this moment was going into shock. I was in shock; my body was in and out of shock as I connected spiritually to the countries. This is what I call geographical shocks my body goes through the same shocks. My heart was weeping for the world. Not everyone knew how severely my body goes through these happenings. Many would not even probably believe me. I am a very grounded person through my practices. I know if I am not grounded, I cannot help anyone. All I know is I get the visions and I need to help those who want my help. I can't help everyone as compassionately as I would like to. People need to want to be helped too, for help to happen, if that makes sense. Many people had gone into conspiracy theories. I was looking into them too, to see if things made sense. I listened and watched. Then I passed on some information to some people I knew, but again it was to question what was going on in our world. WHAT IS GOING ON!

If I can just take you back a moment. I remember on 24th December 2019 my daughter had called me numerous times whilst I was out doing a bit of care work for the elderly. She called me asking for help. She couldn't breathe. Whilst I had a short gap in between calls, I went to see her, she looked dreadful and did struggle to breathe. I called the doctor and they wanted to see her immediately. My husband Daren took Alysha to the doctors whilst I looked after the babies. The doctor said everything was wrong in her body, her breathing, her heart rate, blood pressure, temperature etc. He asked us to take her straight to hospital. Daren did just that and then I handed the babies to their dad, Dylan. I finished my work and went to the hospital as I was so scared for her. She was having slight fits in the hospital emergency bay and she was on a drip and some medication. The staff, Daren and Alysha were wearing masks. I took over from Daren and watched how ghostly pale Alysha looked. The hospital was doing tests on her so we had to wait a little before they transferred her to a side room and told us not to take our masks off.

We waited a few hours and Alysha was quite impatient wanted to be with her babies. It was Christmas eve and she wanted the new baby to have his first Christmas with mummy, so Alysha begged the hospital to let her go home.

I found out from Karen my niece that one of the elderly ladies was in hospital and not good at all. Karen was with the lady for few hours as she had no relatives locally, how sad is this. Whilst waiting for the doctor to come and give us an update I thought to visit the elderly lady who was on the next ward. I asked for permission from the nurses and they said it was very kind of me to visit her. I looked at this elderly lady with such sadness and I blessed her so she could pass over peacefully. I left the ward. Later that evening, I found out the elderly lady passed over half an hour after I had been in. I felt she needed the blessing to leave this incarnation.

I would have preferred Alysha to stay in hospital another day. Alysha came away with many masks and medication, they did say they hoped the tablets would work. They put it down to Type A Influenza. The doctor did say keep the babies away in a different household. So, Alysha came to stay with us and I helped to look after her, parts of the time she was so weak and struggled and some parts she had some energy during the first week. On Christmas day of course the babies came to see their mummy and it was not a normal Christmas by any means. After this we all became unwell and to the point, I struggled to work but I was told I needed to go in anyway due to shortage of staff. I wore my full personal protective equipment to see to the elderly including a new mask that I took from Alysha. I explained to the elderly that I needed to wear the mask for now. I couldn't bear the thought I could pass something on to them. I felt the weakness for some time and it really took some energy to get things done daily.

So, in the coming weeks I was cautious about the new world problem. My two-year-old baby grandson woke up in the middle of the night crying telling his mum SOMETHING BIG IS COMING. And of course, he was right.

～

On the following page is the message I channelled prior to the mass world breakout and world lockdown of Coronavirus, COVID-19.

Dear Precious ones

I want to firstly say please stay safe and well. Please keep self-healing going amidst the unprecedented times we are going through. Those of you who came to The Angelic Healing Reunion in January will know I predicted the mass death we are seeing around the world. I remember saying it was like Hitler effect. But not as a war as a mass thing happening.

I might say it is world war 3 but not a war against nations or people but as a virus world war. It will seem like a war as things will be scarce as we see it. Don't worry and over panic. You will be kept safe. Use your essences do self-healing and I am still here doing your healings.

This is not to worry anyone but for us to be aware something is happening and this is a worldwide lesson to humanity. We must not show greed, we must show compassion to our neighbour, we must work collectively, we must share, there is no need for war.

Our planet is going through massive cleansing, our rivers, streams, canals and oceans will be cleaner in the next 6 months, our air will be cleaner to breathe, our food will be healthy as it grows in the fields, our world is coming to a standstill for a reason. We never took things seriously and compassionately before.

We have never showed real compassion and passion to fellow human beings this is a huge step forward for humanity. Things will get better just ride the storm and remember I said you have to look after yourself, you have to create your own happiness. I am always here for you. Even if you isolate you will not be a lone. I am here for you all.

With Love
Parveen x

During the lockdown we noticed things exactly as in the above message how peaceful the world seemed hardly any aeroplanes in the sky, no noise pollution, you could hear the birds singing, countries were noticing the oceans looking cleaner and more vibrant. During this time, I nurtured my meditation group weekly instead of monthly, what was happening all around us affected everyone, and we needed to keep ourselves healthy and well. Everyone benefitted a lot. We were balanced weekly through the Divine meditations. I constantly reminded the group to stay balanced. Our mental well being was very important as well as to keep safe outside. The weather really helped as we were in spring and summer.

During this period, due to people's requests, I was guided to channel a course to be done via videocall. The angels guided me on this and it was to be called Angels Of Transformation Healing And Service In The New Aeon. It was rather amazing how it came to be. I channelled the course of three levels. I was given visions during this time of how this course will help many people. I was given two scrolls again like I did about fifteen years ago. I was woken up in the night and I had to read them for two hours one night and the same the next night. I wasn't allowed to close my eyes even though I was tired. I was just reading this writing and it wasn't even in English I couldn't see the words clearly, but it was all writing. I had sat for days and days writing and I was given various techniques of healing. Through my excitement I told Lyn about this she said, "Well you have to get on with it." Laughing to myself, yes that's what she always says. I was somewhat concerned at the beginning am I doing the right thing, I don't want to step on anyone's toes. Then it made sense it has to be done. It's an energy needed right now for the right reasons. We need purity. The whole planet is going through changes and we need this now for all. All the teachings were done via videocall and all that attended the courses said it was just as good as in person. Some people would have preferred in person but that could not happen right now due to the pandemic. Much interest came for this new healing modality. Those that came forward wanted to help their clients to feel well and some therapists said they offered different therapies but the winner was always Angels Of Transformation. I was so truly honoured with this new healing system for our new era. I often became so emotional just teaching the courses, it was so much to the level I felt the love of God. The teachings were gentle but transforming. The healing sessions as many said were instant and transformative for all sorts of conditions, from the physical body ailments to mental health support to achieving greater awareness spiritually. There was no time to be wasted, people needed this pure divine healing now. As Lyn said often the angels choose me as I get things done, as I am unafraid. She often said no point choosing her it would take time. We laughed at these conversations. Lyn always gave me moral support, telling me to get on with it. Here we are with a new highly transformative divine energy to support humanity. The angels have guided me for years, I feel so privileged to be the Master of this healing system and many more will join this angelic team. Those who seek help for their journey will feel the amazing love from the masters within the Angels Of Transformation course. A system of healing that is very much needed for the period of change and adaptation we are going through, just perfect! Remember the vision of WINGS OF CHANGE? This was just it. The change was to move to the next level, Angels Of Transformation Healing And Service In The New Aeon was born.

WE ARE ALL VISIONARIES, AND WHAT
WE SEE IS OUR SOUL IN THINGS.
HENRI AMIEL

CHAKRA LOCATIONS

Below is a diagram of where the chakras are based.

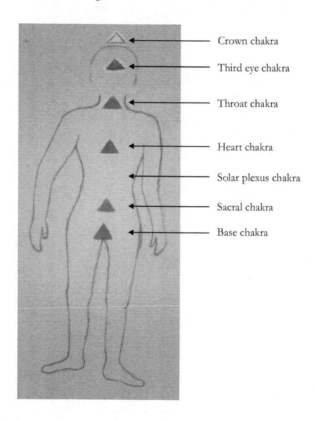

Crown chakra

Third eye chakra

Throat chakra

Heart chakra

Solar plexus chakra

Sacral chakra

Base chakra

AFTER WORD

My spiritual Journey has transformed my life. I am person who loves simplicity. With passion and dedication, I am here to help serve The Divine. My life purpose is clear as I am here to spread the light, to free souls that are trapped and give direction to lost souls. My hunches, intuitions, The Masters and The Angels have guided me further to where I am today. I will continue on saying from my first book Seeing Is Believing, Believing Is Seeing, my many visions have come true. Each event in my life has been carefully placed just like every flower in a garden. Each event is no coincidence. Imagine each flower you place in your garden, that's exactly how The Divine has placed everything for me. Everything has been important for me to recognise. Living in the here and now especially and everything that I was given in my journey I recognised why it happened. I was in the present moment observing my life now and beyond. Looking back, you can see why it happened as this book was written years ago, in 2008, then in 2013 and now the final part is finished for this time in 2021.

~

The stories in this book are accounts of real-life experiences. They are written with utmost, heartfelt honesty by a person who believes in simplicity.

Coincidences? Everything happens for a reason. Parveen's spiritual life stories are is in this book.

Even her healing abilities were not coincidental. Each happening and vision was leading to something greater.

The visions were guidance from the Angels, Ascended Masters and God and it was all happening for a reason. The reason was for transformation.

For those of you whose eyes are closed open them and awaken your soul.

ॐ ॐ ॐ

- The animal spirits come to give us messages and guidance.
- Thank nature for the beauty we have around us and appreciate it. The nature elements need positive energy too.
- The souls that pass over, send them love and be assured they are in the right place. Or seek assistance to help pass souls over.
- Spend time in the moonlight, under the stars and in the warmth of the sun.
- Take time-out meditating, refresh the soul.
- Eat healthily, sleep well and exercise when you can.
- Look after your mind, body and soul.

A SIMPLE MEDITATION TO RELAX THE BODY AND MIND

- Sit or lie down
- Make yourself comfortable
- Close your eyes
- Take in three comfortable deep breaths
- Breathing in gently and rhythmically
- Allow the stress and tensions of the day to leave you
- Allow your body to relax
- Stay in the calm for 5 minutes
- Take three conscious breaths in and out
- Bringing your awareness back to the room
- Affirm 'I am Grounded'
- Wiggle your toes and fingers
- Open your eyes

~

ACKNOWLEDGEMENTS

Angel Guidance Cards
Animal Spirit Guides Steven D Farmer
To My Divine Beings
Angels Of Transformation Healing And Service In The New Aeon
The Scared Doors Of Wisdom Angel Cards
Arnab Deb Christ Image

ABOUT THE AUTHOR

 Parveen runs Pure Meditation Classes on a weekly basis. The classes are on Zoom during the pandemic, and will continue for the foreseeable future. The Zoom Pure Meditation Classes are also very useful for those people who are anywhere in the world. They are enlightening for those whom are awakening to spirituality. Also enriching and enhancing for those already on the spiritual path. The one-to-one meditations are also available through videocall by request.

~⌒

Parveen has always taught angel healings and now Teaches Angels Of Transformation Healing And Service In The New Aeon. From her practice she offers various other therapies to support those who need it.

~⌒

To contact Parveen email: **parveen.angels@yahoo.co.uk**

~⌒

Visit: **www.angelsoftransformation.com**

I cannot make any health claims regarding the complementary therapies that I have discussed in this book. What I can say is that many people have found benefits from the therapies that I offer. Always seek medical guidance for any health problems.

Look out for the next book!

ॐ ॐ ॐ

Printed and bound by CPI Group (UK) Ltd, Croydon, CR0 4YY